LONG TIME NO SEA

SECOND EDITION

Long Time No Sea

A LOOK AT LIFE THROUGH
THE MASK OF A SCUBA DIVER

Second Edition

JEFFREY E. DENNING

© 2022 by Jeffrey E. Denning

Library of Congress Control Number: 2022904201

ISBN (Paperback) 978-0-578-37495-6
ISBN (Hardback) 978-0-578-37496-3

Copyedited by Laurel Robinson

Cover Design and Typesetting by Euan Monaghan

All rights reserved. Except for public domain or source referenced content, no part of this book may be reproduced or transmitted in any form or by any means, electronic or mechanical, including photocopying, recording, or by any information storage or retrieval system, without permission from the copyright owner.

This book was printed in the
United States of America.

Dedicated to my children and the generations beyond:
Know who I am and how I became who I am.
Know who I will be when tomorrow comes
and how who I was became a part of who you are.

Disclaimer

The stories, events, feelings, and emotions
in this book are true. They are stories taken
from my dive logs and journals that span
more than forty years. I added narrative to be
consistent with the spirt of the experience to
enrich my story and make you a part of it.

A special acknowledgment to Patty Mariano Denning,
who gave this story a good ending

TABLE OF CONTENTS

Introduction ix
1. It All Started Here 1
2. The Path From Horseshoe Bay 4
3. The Mom-and-Pop Dive Shop 12
4. Surviving The Big Test 17
5. The Siren of Tilloo 21
6. Abaco Ruth 28
7. Dive on Johnny's Cay 32
8. Stuck in the Mud 34
9. Washed Up on French Beach 38
10. Finding Dead Chest 43
11. Cast Away 46
12. Death Comes to the Dream 52
13. The Rogue Wave 54
14. Dancing With the Sea Lions 56
15. The Flowers of Mimosa Village 58
16. Padre Felipe 65
17. Frances the Nurse 71
18. Anchor's Away 74
19. Lost in the Dark 82
20. My Deepest Dive 84
21. Romantic Octopuses 87

22. His Bride Lost at Sea 89
23. Three Fat Chicks 98
24. The Last Boat Ride 105
25. Remember a Moonbeam 107
26. Sabotaged! 108
27. Flicker in the Night Sky 114
28. Tito, the Boy From Savannah Bight 115
29. The Edge of Wits' End 123
30. Lisa's Secret Profession 129
31. My Dear Friend the Moon 137
32. Shadows in the Sea 140
33. Small Shell From the Sea 145
34. Independence Day 146
35. The Mysterious Mr. Forbes 148
36. The Wooden Boat From Haiti 151
37. Orbit's Canyon 153
38. Those Stupid Dead Plastic Fish 160
39. Revenge of the Seahorse 168
40. Goodbye, *San Sally* 170
41. Conrad 174
42. Sucked Down 179
43. Irma! 183
44. Heart Attack at 50 Feet 198
45. Dolphins on My Bucket List 205
46. I'll Be Right Back 209
47. Nothing os Forever 215

INTRODUCTION

This is a story about how my passion for scuba diving took me on a path where I created and crushed dreams, found love, lost love, sabotaged love, satiated a craving for adventure, walked into and out of disaster, survived the chasms of despair, and was exposed to an enormous amount of wisdom from an unlikely source—Planet Ocean.

I have read numerous stories of other people's life treks and never failed to relate to some aspect of their journeys. There's always something to learn by listening to others, but never have I read about the life lessons people have gleaned by looking through the mask of a scuba diver. In this book, you'll see how I found an intimate connection between man and the world below. I discovered that experience is a chance to taste life, and reflection is a chance to learn from it and fill my path forward with breadth, depth, and vision. In my pondering, I uncovered a richness I probably would not have otherwise found. I saw myself as part of an immensely harmonious universe and discovered how I could easily connect with anyone, anywhere. And I want to share it with you—all of it.

Since 1980 I have taken more than a hundred trips and made more than 1,600 dives. I have been faithful about keeping dive logs and filled a box to the brim with maps, illustrations, scribblings about my feelings and fears, and my interactions with Planet Ocean. For this book I selected forty-seven anecdotes that tell my story that could be similar to yours even if you've never traveled or been scuba diving. You will meet more people than fish. I hope to touch you with my stories of laughing and crying with people I had never met before and whose languages differed from mine. I will take you through the emotional and spiritual brawls that we all experience, and reflect on what I learned and what helped craft the "takeaways" I share in the last chapter. Perhaps in my stories you might see yourself. And that is why I wrote this book.

This is not a book for speed readers. I hope you leave it on the coffee table or nightstand and slowly read each chapter and listen to your reflections after reading mine. How do my stories relate to yours? What "takeaways" do you find that are the same as or different from mine?

In 2007 I published the original version of this book. It was my initial attempt at writing something longer than a two-page Christmas newsletter. Without education in writing fundamentals, it was like building a house with neither plans nor basic carpentry skills. I spent eighteen months trying to find a story in a box of journals typed into a Word document. The first draft was shallow, went nowhere, and sounded like a first-grade "Dick and Jane" book. Then I attempted to add riveting excitement by delving into the technical specifications of how a scuba regulator works, or how the partial pressures of depth and time down contribute to decompression sickness. Did that grab your attention? Didn't think so. When I began weaving the human connection and my reflections into my theme, my story came out of the doldrums.

Reviews from the 2007 edition were encouraging, but I was gutted by someone who thought she was going to read about fish and scuba diving, not disjointed anecdotes of lost love, demons, and the jungles in developing nations. Although I was devastated, it was that poor review that inspired me to revisit the basis of my story and be more mindful of my theme. So here we are.

The day will come when the years will have taken my ability to chase after adventure and all I have to look forward to is musing about my past. Should I not, then, make this journey a most delightful one?

IT ALL STARTED HERE

TRAVEL JOURNAL

Date: August 1981
Location: Phoenix, Arizona

The craving to breathe was overpowering. My chest felt like it was being scorched. I bolted to the surface, gasping for air. The night air swirled deep and filled my lungs. I draped my arms over the side of the pool, ripped off my goggles, and coughed uncontrollably while panting.

I scanned the property and could see most everything, thanks to the August moon with its golden yellow glow. Cicadas buzzed, serenading potential mates with a song so loud that it deafened all other sounds. I pulled the goggles back over my eyes as I hyperventilated to oxygenate my brain. I took and held a deep breath, swam down, and held on to a rock placed in the bottom of the pool to keep me from floating back to the surface.

I was enveloped in silence. All I could hear was the sound of my heart. I turned and watched the moon. Weightlessness freed me. The moonlight became a series of erratic ripples on the surface as it sent ribbons of light dancing around the pool. *I want to stay here forever.* Soon came the want for air. My heart felt like a distant drum that beat rhythmically more and more slowly as I fought the urge to breathe. I defied my body's command to leave this aquatic world; there was more to see and feel. A figure appeared at the edge of the pool and blocked the moon. It was a reminder—I had to go back. How disappointing.

"Are you trying to become a fish?" came the greeting.

I swam to the shallows and was joined by Dottie. We sat half submerged on the pool steps and sipped wine as we watched the night sky. "I could stay down forever," I mused as I pulled Dottie close. "Have you ever been immersed in such romanticism? Can you imagine us watching the moon while swinging in a hammock on some faraway beach instead of here in our backyard?"

"Now, that would sure make a great memory."

"We could go skinny-dipping in the moonlight, and I could sit on the bottom, watching the moon make rippling shadows in the sand. How I wish I could stay down longer."

"All you've been talking about is scuba diving since you came back from the Quota Club trip in the Bahamas last May. Have you ever thought about taking formal scuba diving lessons?"

"Yeah, right. When would I find enough time from my work to do that? Besides, I wouldn't want to do it without you, and you can't swim."

"Maybe we should talk about that, but when you're down there staring up at the moon, what happens to you?"

"There's something magical about being under water, especially in moonlight. The water has a soothing effect. It takes my mind away. When I sit in the deep end clinging to that rock, I disconnect from anything up here. Everything goes away—my worries, my work, having enough money to pay the bills, good and bad thoughts—everything. Down there I am liberated. I can't explain why or how. Maybe it's being weightless or in an environment totally different from ours."

Dottie smiled and snuggled closer. "You know, there's that dive shop on Indian School Road. Maybe we should check it out. I like the idea of sharing a hammock with you on a beach, and if scuba diving will get us there, I'll learn how to swim and even take scuba classes with you."

"You'd do that?"

"I told you long ago I'd go anywhere with you, and if that means going under the water, then let's go."

"How about the Caribbean?"

"And Hawaii."

"We could search for the ultimate hammock location."

"I'll need to go shopping!"

"Shopping?"

"Yeah, I have nothing to wear in the tropics."

"I heard you're supposed to wear little or nothing in the tropics."
"I'll at least need a straw hat with a large brim and a colorful band."
"Yes, that you'll need."
"We can skinny-dip to our hearts' content."
"We'll get a boat to find secluded beaches."
"Who needs seclusion?"
"Aren't we being a little bold?"
"What I do with you is for you, not anyone else."
"It looks like a new underwater world awaits," I said as I waved my hand over the pool.
"Scuba diving sounds scary. I hope I can do it."
"With training, we'll be fine. Besides, I won't let any harm come to you."

We sat in the tepid water, watching the moon drift across the sky. The journey began.

THE PATH FROM HORSESHOE BAY

DIVE LOG

Date: May 1982
Location: Horseshoe Bay, Oahu, Hawaii

Had a sense I was about to get in over my head. Went anyway. When I saw the same sub-aquatic boulder three times, I poked my head out of the water only to find myself on the killer side of the surf zone.

I answered all the preliminary questions honestly. Told them I had been down a few times in the Bahamas. Somehow that labeled me an "intermediate diver." I was directed to the second group of vans. I exchanged polite smiles with others as we waited to head out. A normally convivial and talkative group sat in silence. Was testosterone hiding nervous fear?

Beach Boy Bob appeared. He was to be our divemaster. Very friendly. He was tan with blond hair, had pearly whites and an awesome smile. Asked us our names and how many dives each of us had. I told my story as if to invite myself out of the group but was assured my previous experience was sufficient. Beach Boy Bob described our planned dive—an easy shore entry, a quick swim around the point, and a shallow dive into the catacombs of the lava beds. Sounded exciting. Let's go. The van door slid closed with a solid thump, and we were soon off to the North Shore of Oahu.

A voice in my head became a hammering viper, like the beating of drums on a Roman slave ship at ramming speed. *Get out of the van!* I leaned forward and poked Beach Boy Bob on the shoulder. "You know,

I'm not sure I'm in the right van. I really don't have much experience. Should I have been in the van for first-timers?"

"You'll be fine. We're going to a shallow and easy dive site where it's almost impossible to get into trouble. I checked the conditions early this morning, and they are predicted to stay calm all afternoon. Relax. You'll be OK."

My stomach was yelling something else, but in those days I would frequently dismiss its wisdom. I was, after all, young and immortal. Besides, all new adventures always have some degree of risk.

The silence in our van melted as members began talking with one another, beginning with introductions and what part of the country we were from. We were all part of the brotherhood of the company's Quota Club, a group of overachieving marketing representatives from around the United States who exceeded sales goals. This four-day, red-carpet, first-class trip to Hawaii was the company's reward for top performance. I had recently sold a three-million-dollar computer system to a renowned city in Arizona. That was my ticket.

The vans stopped at Horseshoe Bay, and we poured out. Beach Boy Bob reassembled the group of twelve divers on the edge of the bluff for an orientation. His confidence made it plain that he had been here many times. His voice carried over the noise of the wave action as he gave us a pre-dive briefing. "This group is too large for one dive. We'll draw straws for who will be in each group. When it's your turn, you'll don tanks and gear right here and"—he pointed—"hike along the perimeter to that narrow path that leads down to the only sandy part of the cove—right over there. That's our entry and exit point. We have to time our entry to when the waves are small and break close to shore. That will put us on the outside of the surf zone. Stay alert. We can't linger or we'll get caught inside. I'll lead the way and tell you when it's time to go in. Any questions?"

"Yeah, I have one," said someone. "What's a surf zone?"

Bob pointed to the waves. "See where the waves are breaking? Well, the water between the waves and the shoreline is called a surf zone. That's where those waves churn and froth. We don't want to be in it. That's why we enter from the small beach over there, so we can be on the other side of it. Watch it and you'll see that as the wave action changes, so does the surf zone. With smaller waves, the surf zone is shorter. That's why it's important that we time our entry to make sure we get in when the waves are small. Thanks for asking that question."

I drew the straw for group two and sat on the bluff talking with another diver while watching the first group prepare to go in. He pointed. "Did you know that Sunset Beach is right around the corner? Sunset Beach—you know, the famous winter playground where international surfing superstars take on the 'Pipeline,' where thirty-foot monster breakers can kill those who fail to read the waves wisely."

"Didn't Bob say this dive site was easy?"

"Not to worry, the Pipeline forms in winter, not here in May."

Suddenly, a cry for help came through the pounding sea on the lava cliffs. A diver from the first group must have surfaced and found himself inside the surf zone, and it was carrying him into the jagged shoreline. We scurried down the cliff, but he was too far out of reach. As quickly as the diver was trapped, the waves settled, and he was able to escape a bad fate and exited at the entry point.

Forty-five minutes later, the rest of group one returned. They cackled like chickens about what they had seen. Those of us in the second group helped them out of their gear. Beach Boy Bob and his assistants quickly swapped air tanks.

We donned equipment and hiked down to the entry point. At Beach Boy Bob's instructions, we put on fins and masks and pumped a little air into our buoyancy compensators (BC). He repeated his instructions to enter quickly before the wave action changed. He watched vigilantly. "Let's go!" he commanded, and he quickly vanished between the boulders and under the water. Divers one and two followed. Then it was my turn.

As soon as I was deep enough to swim toward the meeting point, I put my head down and spotted a lava rock covered with green and brown grasses. I swam past it. I saw another rock with the same shape as the first. I continued kicking and, for the third time, saw a boulder of the same size and shape. Something was wrong. I picked my head up above the surface to get my bearings. I looked back to the guys waiting their turn and saw concerned faces. Suddenly... CRASH! A wave broke over my head and a strong surge swept me off.

My attempts to return to the entry point were blocked by surge and frothing waves. The divers waiting behind me backed away, helplessly witnessing my peril. I became a piece of driftwood, being pushed toward the cliffs by an incoming wave and then sucked back into the mouth of a larger one. The waves grew in force, rendering me powerless to rescue myself. A pinnacle popped through the receding water. I grabbed it. In came another wave, which ripped me away—skin and fingernails were left behind, still clawing the pinnacle. Another wave slammed against me and popped open the buckle holding the BC to my body. I sloshed back and forth. Each wave pushed me under and closer to the cliff. I swam back with the returning sea only to be met by another. Somewhere in the bashing, I got separated from my BC and air tank, but I was able to keep a tight bite on the regulator, the part that brings air to my lungs. Without a BC to pull me up, my weight belt pulled me down. I kicked fiendishly toward the surface. I sucked on the regulator, but my demand for air outpaced the gear's ability to supply it. Somehow I managed to climb back into the gear.

Had I been a certified diver, I would have known to let air out of the BC, gone to the bottom, gripped a rock, and waited out the heavy wave action. Or would the panic of my situation have caused me to toss all training aside?

I lost count of how many waves slammed against me, pushing me toward the cliffs. Luckily, I was strong and had the stamina to swim back into oncoming waves, which was better than tangling with the cliffs. But how long could I last? With my strength being sapped, it was becoming a tiring and hopeless battle.

I stopped fighting. The wave action settled. The surf zone shrank, but I was too exhausted to swim back to the entry point. There was not much time left before the waves would pick up and renew their pummeling. My stamina spent, I gave in to the sea. My soul knew it was time to let go. A sense of inner peace overcame me. My fear subsided. My world grew quiet. My thoughts turned to Dottie. She was three thousand miles away. Who would tell her? I whispered a love song, hoping the ever-present connection between us would deliver my final message.

Beach Boy Bob appeared from nowhere and ended my newfound bliss. "We must go in."

"I'm too tired. Can't swim anymore. Think I'll just stay here."

"No, we have to go in before the larger wave sets pick up."

"The jagged cliffs will tear me apart."

"You'll drown if you stay here. We must get out of this before the next set of waves come. Keep your back to the surf and fins up to fend off the jagged lava. I'll be right here with you. Let's go!"

Waves pushed us closer to the cliffs. Sharp pinnacles protruded and then disappeared. I became more afraid of them than of the growing waves. My fins jammed against the lava. Each wave pushed me through the minefield. Bob's technique was working until a wave took my balance and I found myself sloshing around lava like an old rag in a washing machine.

I heard yelling. "Stand up, Jeff. Stand up now!" Rescuers were only a few feet away but still out of reach. With the last bit of strength I stood. "Brace yourself! Here comes another!" CRASH! Down I went. I stood again and took another step. CRASH! Another fall. Another step. Arms reached me, pulling me out. They ripped gear off me. I collapsed. One man from Houston, a muscular volunteer firefighter, threw me over his shoulder and climbed the cliff to a grassy meadow under a tree. So ended my ordeal.

Beach Boy Bob studied me carefully. Through my hyperventilation I apologized for wrecking the dive for the others. Bob put his hand on my shoulder. "Don't apologize for that. You may have saved their lives." He vanished to retrieve two divers waiting on the other side of the surf zone.

My body turned to Jell-O. I was bleeding from the dozens of cuts and slices. My breathing was out of control—too much oxygen. My world spun around at a sickening speed. The hyperventilation cycle had to be broken. One fellow put a paper bag to my mouth and told me to take slow breaths. It worked.

The entire group hustled with a sense of urgency to load the vans and head for the hospital. I lay quietly on the floor. The vans stopped. "Hey, Jeff, we're at a convenience store. Want anything?" Told them I was thirsty. In spite of moaning muscles, I sat up and downed the entire liter of water within minutes. My head resumed its whirling.

Ten minutes passed. I sat up. The world stopped spinning. Muscles began working again. Breathing was back to normal. "Hey, guys. How's it going?" I cheerfully inquired as I bounced up to a seat. They all looked at me in amazement. Bob pulled the van over. Checked my eyes. "I feel fine. Let's go. Skip the hospital."

At the hotel, I hopped out of the van and ignored pleas to see the hotel doctor about all the cuts and abrasions. Was glad to get to my room. I crashed on the bed, thinking I must get proper instruction before ever attempting to dive again.

Lying there felt comforting. I passed out.

BOOM! BOOM! BOOM! I opened the door. The Quota Club program director and a heavyset man with a handheld radio looked at me sternly. "Let's see your wounds," the man with the radio said.

"Come with us," the director said. "You must see a doctor."

"Why? I feel fine."

"Ever hear of staph infection?" the man with the radio asked.

"What infection?"

"You can lose a joint. Are you willing to risk it? You need medical attention. We're going to the hospital."

Medical staff scraped the wounds and studied them with a magnifying glass. They wiped them with peroxide, smeared them with cream, crisscrossed my body with Band-Aids and dressings, gave me a bottle of pills, and issued instructions to come back tomorrow and the day after and the day after that.

By the time I returned to my room, my muscles were in full revolt. Loading up on aspirin was like plugging up a spurting artery with a Band-Aid. I looked to my knee. It felt like someone was whacking it with a large wooden mallet. The adrenaline was wearing off.

Morning was ushered in with a pounding at my door. Fred Winter, my mentor, sales manager, and friend, stood with his usual casual smile. He had come to escort me to the business meeting. Cheers and applause thundered throughout the convention hall as they called my name. "Western Region new account sales executive of the year—1982." Wow! I stood. Peers sitting on the aisle patted my arms as I hobbled past them to the stage. The company's general manager read glowing accolades from video prompters. The story embellished after-the-fact facts, making me the superstar I was not. Blasting lights stalked as I attempted to avoid them. I searched for shadows and lost my balance as my heels pinned down the back curtain. I fell backward and brought the stage curtain down with a crash that made the general manager jump three feet. Accolades were interrupted while stage help rushed in to prop me up. I had waited a long time for my three minutes of glory. There they were. And there they went. I didn't care. I hurt everywhere. I wanted death.

Horseshoe Bay was my life's first whack in the head wake-up call telling me that I was no longer immortal. You'd think that at thirty-eight years old, I would have already learned that lesson. I promised myself I would never dive again without first getting proper instruction and was eager to return home and share it with Dottie.

The Quota Club event ended, and we all dispersed back to dozens of cities across the United States.

Dottie and I sat in the tepid pool water again, and she listened intently as I told the story of my near death at Horseshoe Bay.

"I wonder how many dives it would take for me to know that I should have not gone down," I said.

"Probably none," Dottie said. "You said you were nervous long before going in and you went anyway. That should give you something to think about. Last August we talked about getting scuba lessons. Are you still thinking about doing that, or did your mishap do you in?"

"I would still like to do it, but with my work schedule I never know when I'll be in or out of town. I still think we would have fun with it. How about you?"

"Maybe it's time to visit that dive shop."

* * *

Scuba diving with Dottie had great appeal, but after Horseshoe Bay, I was motivated to learn what level of experience and training it would have taken to safely make that dive. In June 1987, after making 150 dives, three levels of dive certification, and becoming a divemaster, I decided following Beach Boy Bob had been a bad choice. I shuddered at this thought, for the industry defines an active diver as one who makes as few as four dives a year. It's a harsh lesson for those content with trusting the divemaster. For me, two lessons emerged. The first was assessment. Conditions can change rapidly. Tame waters at the beginning of a dive can become an impossible sea upon return. The second lesson was to respect my gut. My stomach had bellowed its objection even after Beach Boy Bob had assured me that all was OK. Since then, I've routinely invited my stomach to the decision table.

In 1989, four experienced divers gathered on the bluffs at Horseshoe Bay. An easy late-morning dive to the catacombs outside the cove. They donned gear, hiked around to the small beach, and prepared themselves for entry. One diver had difficulties and returned to the staging site for repairs after telling his buddies that he would catch up. By the time the fourth diver resolved his problem, the conditions had changed, making entry too risky. He sat waiting, but his buddies never returned. The next day conditions eased, and rescue divers found three bodies pinned inside a catacomb—out of air and cut to shreds. Changing conditions had churned the water into white foam, and they could not find their way out. Trapped inside, they ran out of air.

THE MOM-AND-POP DIVE SHOP

TRAVEL JOURNAL

Date: September 1982
Location: Phoenix, Arizona

The store was eerily quiet. At first we thought we were alone, but then a raspy voice from a woman came out of nowhere. She greeted us as if we were long-lost friends. I looked over my shoulder, certain that she was talking to someone else.

We walked through the back entrance to Aqua Sports, a prominent dive shop in Phoenix, Arizona. To our left was a platform with air tanks. Ahead was a store crammed with scuba equipment. The place smelled like new neoprene just like a tire store smells like tires. To our right was a counter to pay for diving stuff, and just beyond that were three lounge chairs and a small table. There were no racks of T-shirts or dive resort clothing. This was a no-nonsense dive shop.

Dottie and I stood, looking in awe at all the things a person could buy for scuba diving.

"Can I help you?" came a raspy voice from the shadowy corner behind the counter.

I looked for a face. "Yes, we're here to buy snorkeling equipment."

A woman stepped out of the shadow and greeted us with a broad smile. "Are you divers?"

"No. We've snorkeled, but my wife can't swim."

"We dive with our heads, not our backs. You don't need to be much of a swimmer to be a good diver."

The woman ushered us to a wall of dive masks, snorkels, and fins. Then she turned to us. "I'm Rose."

We quickly learned that she was half of this small mom-and-pop business. The banner over the front door boasted "over 35 years in business." Rose's husband, Boris, kept himself hidden somewhere in the back unless he was needed for technical help or diving lore.

There were other dive shops in metropolitan Phoenix, but this one was conveniently close to home. We felt no loyalty going in, but that smiling woman behind the counter created faithful customers in an instant.

"Where are you planning to go snorkeling?"

"We don't know yet. This is our first adventure to a store like this. We've seen pictures of the Bahamas, but that's it."

"What kind of experience are you looking for?"

"Well, we both made our list of features of the perfect place, and our vision of a dream vacation had a boat, clear, warm water, secluded beaches, and romantic sunset dinners. We haven't found such a place yet."

Rose fitted us with basic snorkeling gear. When paying, I asked her if she knew of a place with private beaches and snorkeling. She leaned over the counter and affirmed in a quiet voice as if revealing a well-kept secret, "Well, there's always Bonaire, but you can't beat the Bahamas for sandy beaches and clear, warm water."

That settled it. The Bahamas it was! With that, our new life of adventure under the sun began. And it began blindly by trusting a person we had met only moments before. All we had to do was fill in the blanks about where in the Bahamas we wanted to go and what we wanted to do.

* * *

Rose was gregarious. The majority of her business came from repeat customers. To the diving world, Rose was Mom. Very trustworthy. She was an attentive listener and never engaged in gossip. She knew all the local dirt and never judged anyone. She was a skilled businesswoman. If she did not have what her customers wanted, she called her competitors and asked if they had it. If they did, she'd say, "Great. I'm sending [name and name] to you." Although her competitors always joked about Rose sending people to them, her customers had trust in and loyalty only to her. She knew her customers could find the competition, but she knew they would come back to her first. No one walked out of the store without one of Rose's "throw-in" goodies—such as a small bottle of mask defogger and sunscreen. It fortified customer confidence. She knew that people buy from people, and it was as important to keep old customers as it was to develop new ones.

Boris was an industry icon. He was thin and looked like Jacques Cousteau's twin brother. He was an intense person who took an engineering approach to life. I counted on my fingers to see how old I was when they opened their business. I must have been only five or six when the young Boris organized a group of fellow adventurers, who called themselves the Sand Dabs and made the arduous journey down dusty roads in Mexico that all led to the shores at the Sea of Cortez.

To dive in the fifties, one had to be an inventor, a pioneer. Manufacturers were few. The only dive shops were near water. Choice was limited. Divers made and repaired their own wet suits. There were no gauges to measure remaining air—a diver simply dove until their air supply ended and they flipped a lever on their tanks to give them enough air for a safe ascent. They made their own conveniences. Half of what they brought was gear; the other half consisted of tools and spare parts to fix the constantly failing equipment. When something broke, they took it apart and fixed it. They discarded nothing. Hopelessly broken gear stayed in the spare parts box awaiting cannibalization.

To me, the dive shop was a museum teasing those yearning for travel and adventure. Old relics and new equipment hung like guitars in a music repair shop. Pictures of strange fish adorned the walls. A map of Mexico sat behind the scuba tanks and marked a favorite dive destination with dark blotches from constant finger pointing. Glass display cases left customers slurping with desire. When she got busy with other customers, Rose threw me a set of keys and sent me to check out the new gear in those display cases. In the back was a classroom and storage for rental equipment. In another area beyond that was Boris' machine shop, where he hid all day to invent things.

Honored I was when Boris invited me into the Saturday morning inner circle. I listened to the stories as Boris' friends came into the store one by one, each with a distinct personality. There was the feeling of loyalty and deep, longtime friendships. They became brothers in a lifetime of adventure. So numerous were the stories that repetition was unnecessary. They predated Mike Nelson in the early days of that popular television series *Sea Hunt*, which took hordes of kids like me and filled us with the crazy notion that someday we could be diving like him. I was a man in my thirties, but around Boris and Rose I remained a child with a nickel in my hand and my nose pressed against the glass of the candy store.

I sat in one of the three chairs, but quickly jumped out when one of Boris' friends came through the door. Over the years everything changed, yet much looked the same. Then it was just Boris and me. The others came no more. They were taken as life takes people. Boris sat with feet crossed, arms linked over his head, and gazed into the archives of his yesterdays, searching for another new story. When his feet began to twitch, I fastened my seat belt for another visit to old lore. Over time, the color faded from the pictures on the wall, but the stories were always fresh.

New about-to-be divers came and went. They bought basic gear to snorkel at some dream vacation spot they had yet to find. They signed up for lessons or came in to pick up their much-coveted certification card. And Rose was always the greeter with a warm twinkle in her eye. She was the heartbeat of their business. She made safe her customer's fears. She gave them dreams to dream.

Rose told me stories of the "early days" when their young dive club drove to San Carlos in Mexico and spent a few days camping on the beach, diving and telling stories and basking in good fellowship.

I asked Rose how one knows when their diving days are over. She looked up and away, thinking how to respond. "It's different for everyone. Sometimes diving loses its appeal. Sometimes you lose your dive partner. Sometimes you lose your health. There are a lot of reasons. You'll wake up some morning and discover that your diving days are over. It happens to all of us. You will lose your diving days, but you will never lose your memories of them."

Boris and Rose retired and sold their business in 1993.

Rose left us in 2006. Boris followed in 2016.

Today there remains a building waiting for the steel ball. There is no reference to that mom-and-pop dive shop, Aqua Sports. It has been more than forty years since we walked through the back entrance, yet that momentary image remains as vivid today as then. Rose was a dream maker for others. And thanks to her welcoming smile and engaging interaction, she was a dream maker for us.

SURVIVING THE BIG TEST

DIVE LOG

Date: April 1983
Location: San Clemente, Channel Islands, California

We waited a long time for this dream to come true. We could see into our future. The picture was vivid—warm, clear water, pure white beaches, palm trees, sunsets, watching the moon from swaying hammocks, and sipping rum punches in the late-afternoon breeze. All we had to do was pass the test on this, our checkout dive.

This was our dream? We had spent the night beating against a strong sea and stormy weather to get to this island. The morning brought cold air and heavy gray clouds. There was nothing dreamy about it. I had been diving sporadically for several years and was no stranger to the sport. Dottie, on the other hand, had to have found all this intimidating.

To protect ourselves from the chilly 58-degree water, we each wore a "Farmer John," a thick wet suit that looks like a pair of farmer's overalls. When totally suited, divers can have as much as half an inch of warming neoprene rubber between them and the cold water. Put one of these contraptions on for the first time and you feel like the Pillsbury Doughboy. They also made divers very buoyant. And, without a lot of lead weight, Farmer Johns made it almost possible to walk on water and challenging to keep oneself upright.

Our instructor, a woman from New York whom I nicknamed Bronx, gave us a pre-dive briefing and told us to suit up and jump in.

When we did, icicles slid down my neck into the temperature-sensitive zones of my lower back. Attempts to wiggle it away only made matters worse. Gloomy skies loomed above. Color was nowhere. Cold wind blew through to our bones. Where was the appeal? Why were we here? Is this what we had come for?

We waited for Bronx. Newness became our enemy. We were corks without control. We flailed while attempting to get feet down and heads up. Eventually I figured it out, but Dottie and I drifted apart, and I was unable to get to her soon enough to be helpful. As uncomfortable as it was for me, it had to be worse for her. At least I had some diving experience in clear, warm water. The conditions in this water would make any new diver question the sanity of diving at all.

Dottie remained steadfast and determined to overcome her buoyancy malady. Her attempts to upright herself gave her the appearance of being in trouble. She rested and fought again, but fatigue eventually won.

Bronx leapt into the water and dragged her back to the boat. Perhaps something was attached improperly. I waited in anticipation and concern. Dottie climbed up the boat ladder and disappeared into the warmth of the cabin. Once she was aboard, the instructor turned to me and abruptly ordered me to descend.

"But what's wrong with Dottie?"

"I'll tell you later. Go down."

As I descended, I could feel my anxiety level increase. The world grew darker as we went deeper. Surge washed me back and forth like clothing in a washtub. Finally, I could see sandy patches. Twenty-five pounds of lead held me down as neoprene rubber tried pulling me up. I knelt in the sand, waiting for instructions. Looking around, I could see no color, just shades of dark blue and gray. Cold water continued to trickle down my neck. I was hermetically sealed in neoprene. How could water have seeped in?

Why was Dottie not here? I should have insisted on answers before descending. I was anxious for the dive to end. It was dark, murky, and cold. Visibility was crappy—measured in feet. This was supposed to be fun. *Where's the fun? Who stole the fun?*

My eyes caught the movement of a bright orange fish whose curiosity was greater than its fear of this new intruder. In contrast to the stark blue-gray surroundings, this fellow was a neon sign. A Garibaldi—a damselfish of the Pacific. It must have been nearsighted. It was not content studying me from a distance. It bumped against my mask, poked at my regulator, and cleaned debris from the hair sticking out of my hood. It was the first fish I saw as an about-to-be newly certified diver.

Bronx slapped me on the head to get my attention. We had come down for exercises. Fish watching would come later. We raced through the exercises. Within minutes we were finished. *Let's go play.*

Playing consisted of watching Bronx hunt for abalone. She plunged into a field of seagrass and reappeared with an abalone. I was wondering why she had attached a net bag to my BC. My job was schlepping captured booty. While she hunted, I turned my head to deeper water. *Where's Dottie?*

We swam away from the shallows back to deeper water and ascended on the line attached to the boat. I looked to Bronx. Without my asking, she said, "She's not ready. We'll talk on the boat."

Dottie had "washed out." We never learned why. In my world, "not being ready" doesn't constitute a professional explanation, but it was the only one we got. Dottie and I sat in a warm corner of the boat, trying to piece things together. We had known our confidence would suffer a setback with the new environment, being in a Farmer John wet suit, and the dark weather. *Please, just give us a clue.*

Dottie saw the wheels of surrender turning in my head and encouraged me to complete the open water exercises and earn the diving certificate. Perhaps I had come up this crazy dream, but Dottie had adopted it as hers, and we'd both delighted in the adventurous doors we thought it would open. Now we felt like we'd been expelled. The weather in our spirits was as bleak as what sat over our heads.

The strength of dreams is measured on the great battlefield where unexpected twists and turns test one's resolve and conviction. Our dream was much stronger than Bronx's never-explained decision. Dreams crush defeat. We would just have to find another way.

* * *

We stood at the end of our driveway watching the sun go down as the moon rose big and full at our backs. We always had plenty to say, but on that early evening our silence spoke of a foreboding regret from within. How would we get to our dream? All we had to do was *both* pass the big test. Dottie lamented with a sense of failure. Then she labeled herself a "betrayer." I could feel her piercing hurt.

Light faded, the stars grew bright, and the moon cast long shadows. It seemed that hours went by wordlessly.

"Dottie, being a certified diver is not a prerequisite for our dream."

"How did you know I was thinking about that?"

"We have never been standing out here during the favorite part of our day and been at a loss for words. I know something's been on your mind, and you've been pensive and withdrawn ever since the checkout dive. There's got to be another way to our dream. Let's find it."

We embraced and walked with arms wrapped around each other back to the house. With our spirits propped up, we had a dream to rewrite.

A dream, when driven with passion, is almost unstoppable.

THE SIREN OF TILLOO

TRAVEL JOURNAL

Date: July 1984
Location: Tilloo Cay, Abaco, Bahamas

Three years ago we sat in our pool dreaming about long beaches where we could run like children and bask in the summer sun. The water would be turquoise and warm. We would gently sway in our hammock tied between palm trees outside our remote beach bungalow, watching the billions of stars in the galactic wonder above. We would have a boat to explore secluded islands and coves. We would find this idyllic place in the world and then figure out how to work scuba diving into the vision. Rose, from the dive shop, told us, "You can't beat the Bahamas for sandy beaches and clear, warm water." But there are more than seven hundred islands in the Bahamas.

Before the Internet, finding any dream vacation required a large set of in-the-know contacts, luck, and dogged tenacity. While passing through Nassau a few years before, I had met a man who described a Bahamas island that fit all aspects of what we hoped to find. Before I could get his name or which of the seven hundred islands in the Bahamas he had described, we had to run in opposite directions to catch our planes. Attempting to find the man from Nassau seemed like an impossible challenge, but through a friend of a friend of a friend, I connected with him and got the name and contact for the Abaco Inn on Elbow Cay. A week later I made the phone call, and the wheels of our dream began to turn.

***

The small plane veered left and right as it dodged large, lofty clouds. Below us glowed the turquoise splendor of the Bahamas with water so clear that boats looked as if they were suspended in air. After landing and clearing customs, we rode a rust-ridden taxi to a nearby dock. Our wait felt like hours. Were we on the right dock? Locals assured us a shuttle ferry would soon come and take us to Hope Town across the shallow bay. By the time the boat arrived, many other people and boxes of cargo waited along with us. I studied the other passengers—all were impeccably dressed and adorned in gold bracelets, necklaces, and rings. Menfolk wore their Sunday best. When we spotted boxes with "Abaco Inn" written on them, we knew we were on the right boat. Dottie pointed at them and laughed. "Follow those boxes!"

The ferry made several stops and we remained seated until the "Abaco Inn" boxes were taken off on the main dock. "Wait by those boxes," said the boat captain as the ferry pulled away. "People from the inn know they are here and will come."

We were in the homeland of British Loyalists. We were among their descendants who rejected the American colonists' efforts to resist the British. Their homes were burned, and they were ostracized in their communities for refusing to join the Revolution, and they sought support and protection from their British government in return for their loyalty. Instead, the British sent them to the promised land—the Bahamas—to settle and colonize. History books are filled with the horror stories of their trip and generations of struggling in an impossible land. Over the years they remained remote, untouched, and centuries behind. New homes had the same architecture as those preceding them by two hundred years. Hope Town had no roads. Instead, there were wide grassy walkways straddled by picket fences. The only evidence we saw of vehicles was a single dirt lane with grass growing in the middle and tall grass crowding the sides.

Soon a pale blue van rattled its way down the lane toward the dock. The friendly driver wore a broad smile and announced he was from the "inn" and would do all the lifting. We sat in the van as it bounced and swayed itself out of Hope Town.

We stopped in a clearing next to a single-story building. It had large picture windows all around and a wraparound porch with a stone floor and a half dozen tables and chairs. This out-of-the-way resort could accommodate six or eight couples. Its main house overlooked the Atlantic on one side and the Caribbean on the other. A gazebo and pool kissed the edge of the ocean as waves sometimes crashed against the rocky cliffs, sending plumes of spray skyward, washing the gazebo and anyone standing in it.

Two young managers welcomed and escorted us down a long, quiet, winding path protected by palms and large vegetation. The farther down we went, the narrower the path and lower the canopy. Hermit crabs rustled dead leaves in a scurry to safety. The floral cover opened, and the sound of the sea and breeze caressed our faces. We were there, in Bungalow 6. It was to be our home for the next ten days.

We asked about Ruth, the inn's owner and romantic legend. "She's off island and will be back in a few days," said the manager.

We rented a seventeen-foot Boston Whaler with a small but powerful outboard motor. It had a middle console with seat, a blue Bimini top for sun shelter, and a small foredeck with under-seat storage. Boat orientation was brief. "These boats have a reputation for durability and reliability. You could cut it in half and both pieces would continue to float."

Since everyone in the islands owns a boat, no one ever thought we needed to know anything more than that a large orange buoy marked the channel to the inn. Marina staff waved as they sent us off, unaware that they had just rented a boat to people who knew nothing about basic nautical skills such as draining the boat of rainwater, bleeding air from the fuel lines, lifting and locking the motor, "beaching" the boat, or anchoring.

Our first exploratory adventure shattered our already faltering confidence when our propeller went *clank-clank-clank* on a piece of coral in water we thought was deeper.

"Go south to Tilloo," the locals said the next day. "It's a huge sandbar in the middle of nowhere. You can't miss it. Just head south and you'll run right into it." We were a little sensitive to their choice of words, "run right into it," especially the day after our coral encounter.

With pounding hearts and dry mouths, we headed south for Tilloo. Thirty minutes later a blue sliver of brightness appeared in the distance. Very distinctive against the dark waters. Was that Tilloo? As we drew closer, it got larger and transformed itself into a bright turquoise beam that began to encircle us. With motor at full stop, we drifted over it. We used our oar as a sounding device. The depth looked like two feet, but the oar could not find the bottom. Water clarity deceived our judgment of depth.

Tilloo—there was nothing to it. It was just a sandbar in the middle of nowhere and close to a long, narrow cay. Surrounded by a sea darkened by eelgrass, it was shallow and magnificently simple. The bottom looked like a desert scene—whitewashed sand with small ridges rippling with the cleansing current.

On Tilloo, there were few fish, and there was no coral, no seagrass. Nothing. Nothing but the skeletal remains of thousands upon thousands of sand dollars sticking up like vanilla wafers in a scoop of ice cream. The sweeping current continuously moved sand back and forth—bringing the sand dollars up from their sandy graves.

Tilloo became our daily Mecca that left us with a treasured memory. Upon returning home, people asked how we had spent our days. "Well, after breakfast we motored our little boat to a far-off sandbar and anchored there most of the day. There was nothing to do but soak in the sun and dive down for sand dollars."

"That's it? That's all you did? Sounds boring."

We had a different perspective.

***

During the summer months, squalls were as common as four o'clock. Not knowing how to handle them, we'd keep a close eye on approaching storms and race for home if we thought one was becoming a threat. After Dottie and I had run from squalls for three days, locals taught us how to "beach" the boat near shore, but it was up to us to gain enough experience to distinguish between a small "sit-it-out" squall and a "run-from-it" mother storm.

I was up at dawn to snap a picture of clouds far to the east with the sun piercing through their holes. At breakfast, the line on the eastern horizon was distinctly dark, but locals told us not to worry—it was far off and "hanging out there." Still, we did not trust our instincts and headed back for lunch and to see if the skies changed. The locals were right. It was just going to hang out there.

Back at Tilloo after lunch, I harvested sand dollars for a collage we had decided to make as a commemorative plaque of our trip while Dottie spread them out to dry on the boat's gunwale. We gathered hundreds of them, knowing many would perish on the long journey back to Phoenix. The water was tepid. The sun warming. Tilloo was intoxicating. We were lured to sleep.

I awoke with a start. The warming sun went out like a light. The breeze brought cooler air. Tilloo turned gray. I sat up, struggling to regain alertness. The storm was eminently upon us. We headed for a nearby cay, lifted and locked the engine, threw out a stern anchor, and secured a front line around a palm tree. There! We were ready. Bring on the squall! We sat in chest-deep water. As the wind increased its intensity, palm fronds slapped one another and sounded like applause. Tilloo became frothy. No worries, we were protected in the lee.

Our confidence faded as distant boats scurried north to safety. What did they know that we didn't? Maybe we were losing valuable time sitting on the beach. What if the storm came back on us? Filled with self-doubt, we headed back to the inn.

The wind was at our backs. This was good. But when we rounded a point on a barrier cay, the picture changed. Sea chop rose to short three-foot slamming waves, and the wind came strong to our beam. Ahead we could see the top of the sea turn white as a gray wedge of rain pushed ahead of the wind. It enveloped us. The wild wind lifted the bow and pushed it downwind—heading straight for another cay surrounded with a protective coat of sharp limestone and coral. I wrestled with the wind to get back on course, only to be thwarted again and again and again.

The conditions were getting serious. How could such a shallow bay develop such rage? Wind sliced off the tops of the waves, creating a blasting nozzle of razor-sharp white water. It stung, but I had to keep an eye out to find the orange buoy.

The boat ride between the inn and Tilloo was usually a half hour, and we had long since passed that time. I was lost and felt forced to head to the protection of an adjacent cay. Its shoreline, too, was protected by treacherous limestone, but at least there was no chop and sharp spray. When facing the dark protruding monoliths, I knew being there was not such a good idea.

From the corner of my eye I spotted the orange buoy and turned to the safety of depth but back into the harm of the squall. As wild as the conditions were, there was a sense of comfort in knowing we were near the orange buoy and thus far had managed to keep the boat upright. We turned into the full force of the squall and headed toward what we hoped would be the channel. As we neared the cay, the intensity of the wind and chop diminished. We spotted the day markers at the inn, and that helped keep us in the center of the narrow channel.

Later we were told the storm was the worst they had seen in years. And we survived it? When we told locals how we had prepared for it, they assured us we had done the right thing but should have stayed on Tilloo. Getting caught in the squall was a nail-biter and a confidence builder. After that day, we became fearless to the threat of squalls.

Ruth, whom you will meet in the next chapter, was the inn's owner and liked mixing up dinner seating assignments and paired us up with Alex and Dianne. They became fascinated with our stories of Tilloo and asked if they could accompany us. We told them they were welcome, and explained that we spent our days skinny-dipping. If that offended them, perhaps they would rather not come. They shrugged and joined us. Neither Dottie nor I had ever willingly done this before, but whatever trace of self-consciousness was once there had now vanished.

The angle of the sun made Tilloo glow. Our guests watched with anticipation as Tilloo appeared on the horizon. They, too, were drawn into its magical spell. The sun raced across the sky, each moment changing the color and mood of Tilloo. We were mesmerized and drunk with relaxation.

The sandy bottom was only five feet below. Dottie decided to try her hand at sand dollar gathering. She slipped into the water and quickly spotted a large one, yelled through her snorkel, dove down, and grabbed it. She flew to the surface with the sand dollar over her head as if she had just discovered a gold doubloon from a Spanish galleon. We all cheered with excitement and delight. I held Dottie and swirled her around as we celebrated her find and her ability to get down under.

"You two are lost. You're in a world of your own. You are both a delight." Words that met us as we climbed back into the boat amidst celebratory Kodak moments.

It was a great day, one of our best, and it was time to leave. We returned to the inn slowly, reluctant to let go of Tilloo.

Once back home, we made the collage of sand dollars—our freeze frame of history and a collection of memories. And Dottie's sand dollar? Only I remember which one it is. And if age takes my memory, I'll just point to another.

At Tilloo we found freedom. Freedom from distraction. From inhibition. From the complicated world that awaited us. Freedom to escape. Freedom to rediscover each other without interruption. And freedom to focus on what mattered. We brought it home. It became our life. It was part of a long day we thought could never end.

ABACO RUTH

TRAVEL JOURNAL

Date: July 1984
Location: Elbow Cay, Abaco, Bahamas

We headed toward Johnny's Cay, a tiny island that was out of the way and devoid of humans. While swimming in the channel and far from the security of our boat, we found we were not as alone as we thought.

On the third day of our Abaco visit, the manager pointed us to Johnny's Cay, which had a long, shallow, sandy beach and a nearby channel that boasted good snorkeling. "It's very private. No one ever goes there. You'll have the whole place to yourselves." We anchored, stripped naked, grabbed snorkeling gear, and drifted over to the channel. And then we heard the buzzing of an approaching boat. So much for "no one ever goes there." Splash! Several snorkelers jumped off their boat and came our way. If you ever unexpectedly find a group of strangers between you and your clothing, just start speaking French. Except for one, the group passed us without noticing. A woman swam toward us. It was as if she were trying to intercept us. She had a broad smile and was quite friendly. And she was half as naked as us. "You must be Dottie and Jeff. Hi! I'm Ruth."

That's how we met Ruth, the mysterious myth whose name echoed the song of the islands. Ruth was our hostess and owner of the inn. She was a handsome woman filled with zest, sure-footedness, and a quick taste for romance and adventure. She punctuated her life with flair. Legend had it that she had bought the inn with her lover and transformed it into a place to watch sunsets with flamboyant grandeur. There was a significant age difference between them that Ruth managed to overcome through attitude and attention to her mate. But her "other" was frequently stateside on business, leaving Ruth too long, watching the sunset alone with a flower in her ear, waiting for him to come home.

One day he never returned. Ruth, though, remained hopelessly loyal to her romantic ways. And therein is the magic that is the rest of this story.

***

Ruth oozed romanticism. She talked it, walked it, dressed it. Her every thought was sensuous. She was aware of herself and of the woman within. Ruth was a very sexy woman in her fifties and thought the Islands should outlaw clothing altogether. Said it was restrictive, allowed a person to hide, and that masked the flavors of life. Clothed people cannot experience or know themselves. They live in fear of self-discovery. And that fear causes them to hide more. There was circularity in her philosophy, but this was the world according to Ruth.

Ruth's personal mission was to help liberate all women by safely introducing them to the gift of self-awareness. Her quest was for women to be sensual not for others, but for themselves. Being appreciated by others was only a pleasant side effect.

Ruth epitomized the expression "walk the talk." It was her way to lure her women guests into test-driving "sensuousness," nicely packaged in a risk-free environment. No extra charge.

When Ruth was present to welcome and orient new guests, it went like this: "Down by the pool there is a gazebo for sunrises, moonrises, afternoon wine, and lethargic wave watching. There is a private area for those wishing to get a full body tan while being intoxicated by caressing zephyrs whispering gently off the summer sea. There is the swimming pool overlooking the sea where you can experience the sensuousness of après-dinner skinny-dipping. Oh, and down those pathways over there are the rooms."

By week's end women were skinny-dipping in the light of the moon or sitting topless in the shallow pool, sipping a late-afternoon fruity drink topped with colorful paper parasols. They ignored others and grew comfortable with themselves. Their menfolk seemed accepting of the new *her*. Brassieres were left in the cottages and blouses left blatantly unbuttoned. While creating a safe place to test this risky voyage, it was plain to see Ruth's plan was grabbing hold of her guests.

Ruth approached Dottie. She crossed her arms, studying her with an artful eye. "You're not wearing much clothing, and this is good, but we need to make a few changes." Dottie had a quizzical *What do you have in mind?* look on her face. With the flick of her finger, Ruth quickly released a few buttons on Dottie's blouse, pulled the top open, pulled the collar up, and then threw a string of heavy brown beads around her neck. Ruth stood back, hands on hips, cocked her head, and with an approving grin proclaimed, "There, now you're gettin' it!"

* * *

After breakfast one day, Dottie stood boldly in the doorway of our cottage clad only in her panties. With one hand leaning high on the doorway and the other on her hip, the image of her became indelible. There was the smile of confidence, independence, and self-awareness. During that holiday, Dottie became a carbon copy of Ruth's attitude. When we went back home, she cast aside clothing, dressed sensuously when we went out for dinner, and transformed at-home meals into romantic experiences through music and candlelight. She suggested framing and hanging our island pictures in our bathroom, bedroom, and partially down the hall. It extended our summer holiday throughout the year, she reasoned. "You won't mind when company sees half-naked pictures of you?" I asked.

She shrugged. "Who cares? Besides, it's not for them."

We brought the islands home with us. Each day after work, Dottie greeted me at the door with a welcoming smile. She adopted the island dress with one of my retired business dress shirts, sleeves rolled up, unbuttoned halfway to her waist, and a colorful sash for accent. We stood outside enjoying each other's company as we watched the sun set behind the black silhouettes of distant palm trees and the moonrise enshrouding us in its golden light. These times could have lasted forever, but that could never be anything more than a fantasy.

At one time I allowed others to influence my life by what I thought they might think of me. Maybe it's upbringing. Still, there is no tasting, no feeling, no experiencing of self while looking over one's shoulder to see who may be watching, judging, or disapproving. It is a malady that, fortunately, we can overcome with attitude and practice.

In 1994 I made a pilgrimage back to the Abaco Inn. Ruth had long since sold it to another romantic.

DIVE ON JOHNNY'S CAY

TRAVEL JOURNAL

Date: July 1985
Location: Elbow Cay, Abaco, Bahamas

After Dottie's 1983 certification washout in the Channel Islands, our local dive shop gave me as many tanks as I requested to go over the water exercises again and again until Dottie could do them without thinking. When we thought she was ready, we arranged for Bronx to give her a personal checkout in our pool. Bronx promised that if she passed, she would give Dottie a referral letter so we could get her air tanks in the Bahamas.

I sat quietly on the pool deck as Dottie and Bronx descended. Bubbles boiled to the surface. Ten minutes passed. Then fifteen. Thirty minutes passed. *Things must be going well.* The bubbles moved from the deep to the shallow end. They stood and Bronx yelled a congratulatory "Hooray."

The rules for diving in the Bahamas differ from those in the United States. Negligence notwithstanding, Bahamas dive shops didn't seem to be as fussy about a person actually having the skill. Dottie's referral letter was enough to get her a tank.

We were told we should head for Johnny's Cay and dive the thin channel between there and Man-O-War Cay. It was a short swim to the shallow dive site. Little fish were plentiful, and we would always be close to shore.

We reviewed our plan, donned gear in three feet of water, and followed the bottom contour down to deeper water—eight feet below the surface. This was an exciting moment of truth—Dottie remained relaxed and seemed to be enjoying herself.

The tide raced through the small cut between our starting point and Man-O-War Cay. Had to hold on to dead coral to keep from being swept away. Dottie's hair waved wildly in the current. Her anxiety levels could have soared, but she appeared surprisingly comfortable.

When we got back to the boat, Dottie, excited about her accomplishment, ripped her wet suit off, lunged at my neck, and dragged me back into the water. I thought, *If this is how all dives are going to end, this will prove to be a fun sport.*

STUCK IN THE MUD

DIVE LOG

Date: October 1985
Location: Butcher Jones Beach, Saguaro Lake, Arizona

Air was released from the lift bag, and the I-beam sank to the muddy bottom fifteen feet below. Bobby and I watched from the shoreline, poised to locate and bring it back to the surface. In my efforts to help my buddy, the training exercise came within moments of becoming a tragedy.

With my Horseshoe Bay experience three years behind me, my thirst for training remained fresh. I signed up with three others for advanced scuba lessons with specialties in limited visibility diving, search and recovery, deep diving, and self-rescue.

For all the water exercises, Bobby was my assigned buddy. He was a slight man—thin and not much taller than five feet. Throughout the training period we got to know each other well. It was difficult watching him struggle with severely alcoholic parents who, he told me, were constantly promising to show up and frequently too drunk to stand. Still, Bobby remained unconditionally loyal to them. Although I once had my own troubles with an alcoholic parent, they paled in comparison with his. I overflowed with empathy, but he didn't know we were kindred spirits, and I never reached out. Why I stood back and watched is something I will question for the rest of my life.

Bobby and I stood on the shores of Lake Saguaro one hot Saturday morning. The thought of getting that water in our mouths was enough to make us clench the regulator in our teeth hard enough to bite off the mouthpiece. We were about to embark on a "search and recovery" training exercise required for advanced certification.

Our mission was to locate and refloat a one-hundred-pound, four-foot-long steel I-beam. The exercise would combine our skills of navigation, team coordination, object retrieval, zero visibility diving, and knot tying. We had to triangulate on a sunken object, find it, tie balloon-like lift bags to it, and bring it to the surface.

Bronx and her assistant floated the I-beam out to a designated location about a hundred feet offshore. We had ten seconds to get a compass bearing before they let air out of the lift bags. Then we had to go retrieve it.

Bobby and I stood about fifty feet apart, which made our compass headings different. For me, it would take twenty-five kick cycles to go the hundred feet—four feet per kick with left and right fin. All we had to do was pay attention to our compass heading and count our fin kicks. If we did it right, we'd meet at the same time and bump into the I-beam.

Practicing the exercise in a crystal-clear warm-water pool was much different from being in Lake Saguaro. We wore full wet suits for the 72-degree water, but the air temperature was 90 degrees, which turned the wet suits into sauna suits. The deeper we went, the murkier it got. Without visibility I could not see rocks or other references to keep me from straying off course. I kept my compass pointing in the intended direction and my mask pressed down onto the compass.

Crash! I recoiled, then inched forward, feeling my way around a metal basket with wheels. *Settle down, buddy,* I thought. *You almost freaked out over a grocery cart.* I took a deep breath and resumed my task, but I had lost count of my kick cycles. I had kicked about fifteen cycles—or was it thirteen? or sixteen? I blew the exercise; meeting Bobby would be accidental.

I decided I had made fifteen kick cycles and swam until reaching twenty-five. I waited for Bobby. A minute passed. No Bobby. I initiated the lost buddy procedure and surfaced. Bobby's bubbles were only a few feet from me, but in that visibility it may as well have been a mile. I followed his bubbles down and we reconnected. There was no I-beam nearby. We surfaced to discuss options and plan B. We dove back down, locked arms, and began swimming in patterns. We got lucky.

We went to work on phase two—securing and refloating the I-beam.

We worked at opposite ends to get a line around the I-beam and tighten it enough so it would not slip off. There was an incredible suction in the soft mud. I plunged my hands into the muck and could not tell water from mud. The deeper I dug, the thicker and colder it felt. My entire arm was inside a vat of thickening ice cream. It took great effort to overpower the suction of the mud and wrap the line tight and two times around the I-beam. A loose line would allow the I-beam to slip back into the mud if the lift bags were not evenly filled. I did not want to have to do this again. Having bugs with long, hairy legs crawl on my face would have been preferable.

My end was ready. *How's Bobby doing?* He was struggling to get the line under his end of the I-beam. Since Bobby was a slight man, he would have difficulty overcoming the suction. *Let me help you, buddy.*

I became an octopus prying open a clam. Through strain and persistence, the I-beam gave way in the mud. Felt like I was up to my knees in stirred-up muck, and the bottom darkened as it mixed with the water. There was not even enough light to read the gauges. Flashlights would do no good. I looked to the surface, fifteen feet away, but all I could see there was the glow of chocolate milk. It was quiet and I suddenly felt very alone. The energy it took to lift Bobby's end made me uncomfortably hot, and I was breathing air faster. I became concerned about having to abort the exercise because of my running low on air.

With Bobby's end of the I-beam off the bottom, I gave him ten seconds to wrap a line around it before the pressure on my back forced me to set it back down. I patted Bobby on the shoulder to let him know I was going back to finish preparation on my side. I was gratified, knowing I had rescued my buddy from the weight of the beam.

I pulled out a lift bag rolled tightly and clipped to my buoyancy compensator, secured it to the line around the I-beam, and filled it with enough air to make it float. As the mud settled, visibility revealed a faint yellow lift bag that looked close and far away at the same time. Very creepy. My end was ready.

I moved to Bobby's side, only to discover he had made no progress. It seemed like such a simple task. What was taking him so long? In class, we had gone over it again and again. We had practiced in the dark. *Why is he no farther along?*

I felt around. Bobby was still trying to wrap the line around the I-beam. That should have been done long ago when I held it up. I ran my hands down his arm, only to discover that both his hands were stuck under the I-beam and he didn't have the strength to free himself.

I was amused at first, but then thought of the horror if Bobby had lost his regulator or had freaked if his mask filled with muck. I was only a few feet away. Bobby could have died, and I would not have known soon enough to make a difference in the outcome. Humor gave way to the thought of ugly possibilities.

I helped Bobby finish his end. We coordinated a slow and controlled ascent to keep the I-beam level. Minutes later the water became lighter, and suddenly we broke the surface with the I-beam securely attached. My eyes went from seeing nothing to being bombarded with infinite distance. Once the mental confusion subsided, I celebrated. We passed.

In all my dives that followed, few were as nerve-racking as the search for that I-beam. With visibility at zero and light fading, it would be easy for a person to "lose it" down there, but in those days there was little that I found intimidating. Today I no longer have to prove anything to anyone, not even myself. I doubt that I still have the "right stuff" to do anything like that again.

Two of us went down that day. Bobby got stuck in the mud and lost the use of his hands. Had the regulator fallen from his mouth or his mask filled with muddy water, it could well have resulted in a tragic end. As I went about my business feeling gratified because I'd "helped" my buddy, he could have perished less than a few feet away from me. And his death would have been my doing.

Our lives can change forever in an instant, triggered by incidents small yet powerful.

In the confusion and chaos in our own worlds, it is easy to become sightless by that which colors our perceptions. I shudder whenever I see the image of Bobby stuck in the mud. The Lord sent an army of angels that day to keep him calm in his helplessness. Once Bobby was safe, they started working me over. *What more proof do you need to be convinced that this rescuer tendency in you is more destructive than beneficial?*

That Saturday morning on Butcher Jones Beach, I realized that getting stuck in the mud is an expected part of life, not hapless misfortune in need of a savior. But more importantly, when it is rescuing I have in mind, the best rescue is encouragement and compassion, so others find the strength and the light to rescue themselves.

WASHED UP ON FRENCH BEACH

DIVE LOG

Date: November 1985
Location: French Beach, San Carlos, Mexico

While learning the "ropes" of dive training, I discovered that there was something far more important than skills and technique.

When I had completed my advanced dive certification and made about sixty dives, I was asked about my interest in instructing. I beamed with the invitation and jumped right in. After sitting through several classroom sessions, I was asked to begin a new class under the close supervision of the head instructor, Bronx.

On the first night of class we asked students what lured them to diving. Answers varied, but the ones that were the most worrisome came from women motivated by an obsessive need to please their menfolk. I cringed when I heard this. "Because of him" constitutes the worst reason for learning how to dive. "Because of him" told me these women were susceptible to mates who managed relationships through control and intimidation. I grew to detest this bully attitude that men inflict on their mates. This "dive or else we're through" threat left many a woman disfigured for life, and when their marriages slammed into the cliff, they most likely were blamed for its failure. What they ever saw in these scoundrels continues to evade me. There, I got that out of my system.

Throughout the class, Sarah heaped pressure upon herself to do well. While I graded her assignments, she stood by and nervously commented, "Be kind to me. If I don't pass, my husband will divorce me." At first I chuckled, but at each segment of the class she made the same comment. If she had taken up diving to save her marriage, then hers was already teetering on the brink of ruins.

I shared my concern with Bronx, who admonished, "Do not rescue her. You tend to do that. She must be independently capable of accomplishing all the exercises. If you were to act as rescuer, you would be responsible for developing weak divers and, worse, leaving them ill-prepared to handle an emergency that could result in their own death."

Swirling in my head was my unasked question, *What about helping them step through their fears?*

Sarah's husband... Never met him. Never wanted to. Already disliked the bastard. This sense of "perform or perish" impairs learning. And living. While doing her class prerequisite swim test, Sarah was a fish. But put a tank on her, and you'd have thought it was her first time in water. Difficult as it was, Sarah performed all the exercises and homework assignments, and did well on her written examination. All she had to do now was pass the open water evaluation.

All I knew about Sarah was what I observed in class. She was a middle-aged woman with an agreeable voice and a gentle manner. She avoided eye contact and seemed like a person who would swiftly acquiesce in a conflict. In the group, she was not an initiator but a warm supporter. Always very willing to please and constantly sought approval. I thought she was a sitting duck for the likes of bullies.

* * *

French Beach is a cove north of San Carlos, Mexico, in the Sea of Cortez. It was a grueling eight-hour drive from Phoenix, and the last few miles involved dusty, bumpy roads, thick cactus, scorpions, snakes, and range cattle with big horns. From the top of the hill overlooking the beach one could see for miles up and down the coastline, a view that would make you want to run right into the water, no matter how cold it might be. The region was bone dry, devoid of pollution, and always hot to downright scorching hot. It was in the southern half of the Sonoran Desert, one of the most alive and beautiful deserts in the world. French Beach was protected from the ravages of the Sea of Cortez and had easy shore access, making it a primo location for teaching.

***

The students listened to the briefing and dealt with personal anxiety over their first "official" dive in the ocean. When given the word, they set up their tanks, donned wet suits, and carried everything down to the shoreline. They swam out without weight or tanks to perform their first open water session—"skin diving"—which included snorkeling, attempting to dive down to retrieve a rock or sand, and practicing saving or assisting tired divers.

Bronx used this experience as a comical introduction to scuba diving in "open water," meaning something more vast than a swimming pool. Wearing thick neoprene rubber and no weight belts made diving down almost impossible. With all the flailing and cheering when one diver actually got under water, the distraction eradicated almost all anxiety.

The second dive was the students' first dive using scuba. They swam about 150 feet to a sandy dive site in fifteen feet of water. Upon Bronx's word, all divers descended one by one down a line.

On this trip, my job was shore patrol to ensure personal belongings and equipment did not vanish while the students were down.

No sooner had they descended than the entire group surfaced and huddled. They had surfaced much too soon. I watched from a distance and could only speculate. There must have been a problem.

Bronx yelled for me to don my wet suit and swim to them. When I arrived, she pointed to a distressed diver and said, "Take her back!"

I towed the diver ashore. I could sense devastation. She floated on her back, allowing me to do all the work. With her mask and hood in place, it was difficult to know who I was bringing back to the beach.

You don't have to guess. My charge was Sarah.

I dropped her gear at the water's edge and helped her to the staging area and peeled off her wet suit.

Sarah sat staring out over the water as she caught her breath. She threw her mask down in despair. Whatever had happened was plain—it meant failure and was probably her last dive on this trip.

Sarah dropped her head, covered her face, and began sobbing.

I knelt beside her. She looked up and threw her arms around my neck as she went into a full-fledged ugly cry. My eyes filled with tears.

"It's all over," she repeated as she clenched my shoulders and buried her head in my chest.

I foolishly tried to soothe her. "Sarah, you can take the class again. Many students don't do well on their first open water class."

"No, it's not the class that's all over. My husband is going to divorce me. He told me to come home certified or not come home at all." And she fell deeper into the gnawing blackness of what she had to face when she returned to Arizona.

Sarah had not come here to learn how to dive. She had come to save her marriage.

By the time the other students returned, Sarah had settled down. We ate lunch during the surface interval while waiting for the second dive.

Sarah sheepishly approached Bronx. "Take me out during lunch. I know I can do it. Please." Her petition failed. Bronx looked over the water with steely eyes and folded arms and said, "No." Her rigidity left a disquieting silence on the beach.

There were no explanations for what caused her to wash out. I inquired and was warned not to become the rescuer.

Sarah sat out the afternoon training session. She sat the next day out while watching the other students celebrate their personal accomplishments. Nothing was said between her and Bronx—not a single word since her ill-fated appeal the previous day.

I could not help thinking about the timing of Bronx's unyielding alliance to rules and the insensitivity to the human side of teaching. Being washed out had significant, life-changing implications for Sarah. But then, Bronx was a professional and skilled at providing by-the-book comprehensive training. Sympathy had its place, and putting home-front relationships ahead of safety was not part of the program.

***

When Dottie and I began private lessons years before, her response to the "why do you want to dive" question was "To be with Jeff, of course." Did that make me a bully? Was what I hated in Sarah's husband really a disdain for self? And was my tearful empathy for Sarah born out of the pain I caused Dottie when she washed out, leaving her with the same sense of failure? These thoughts troubled me until I was in a position to compensate for what I sometimes thought were counterproductive teaching methods by Bronx.

After co-teaching with Bronx for two years, she began separating students from the class who were unable to keep up and asked me to take them to a different part of the pool for private instruction. Before the night's session ended, my "problem" students returned to the group better prepared for the next session than their fellow students. Part of the success was the result of the intensity of personal one-on-one instruction, and part was my sheer determination to prove that there was something more flawed with the system than with the student.

We don't all learn the same way. Sometimes a one-size-fits-all system doesn't always fit all. It is unfortunate that we are too quick to expel those who "can't keep up"—those whose learning preferences are slower. The corporate world is no more forgiving. That environment, after all, is more shark infested than what most divers will ever see under water.

Before leaving you with a sense that Bronx was the monster and I the dragon slayer with a better cause, recognize that our clash was mostly the result of differing styles. Bronx was tough minded, disciplined, and demanding, and paced the class for students who rapidly became comfortable with the new experience. She finally came to the realization that remedial one-on-one catch-up training was not pampering, and my style kept the slower students on board.

The fundamental skills I learned in the early 1980s guided me on the 1,600 dives that followed. Although hardened and militaristic in her approach, all those certified under Bronx were well prepared for a good, fun, and safe diving experience.

In the following years while I was a co-instructor, no other student washed out of the program for unexplained reasons. Warnings constantly came, however, about being the rescuer. Maybe I was. But then again, we all need a little rescuing from time to time.

I never heard about Sarah again. She may have gone home to a divorce. That is, if she was lucky. I felt it was her only path to emotional rehabilitation.

Encouragement has always been far more effective for accomplishment than threatening others with failure. A dream is only a moment away—waiting just on the other side of that thin wall of fear.

FINDING DEAD CHEST

TRAVEL JOURNAL

Date: May 1986
Location: British Virgin Islands

When my gear didn't show up in the baggage reclaim area in St. Thomas, I was sure I would never see it again.

I had signed up as a subject on a medical research diving trip. Afterward, I would meet up with Dottie in the Abaco Islands. When I arrived in the British Virgins without gear, one of the other medical subjects on the boat became a maddening broken record about how it would never be recovered, that it had already been parsed out in the black market. "Stolen dive bags," he said with certainty, "sell for five hundred dollars unopened." I had waited a long time for this trip, and now it seemed over before it had even begun. I fretted so much, I got almost no sleep that night.

Captain Tim took me to a storage locker on the boat. He opened it, displaying a smorgasbord of rental dive equipment that they offered at no charge. He even threw in a boat T-shirt for body protection. At least I had my own mask.

We dove using the US Navy Air Dive Tables. This medical research trip was to study the effects of "silent bubbles" in advance of a newer and more conservative set of recreational dive tables. The research not only resulted in revised bottom times, but also established a baseline for something that would later shape a new rage in the diving industry—dive computers.

I dove using the boat's gear and never missed my own. Why had I spent so much time gathering, sorting, and preparing to bring all that stuff when I could have used boat gear?

* * *

Captain Tim summoned me to the inflatable boat, and we headed for a tiny island called Dead Chest. We zigzagged around other islands, through cuts, and over shallows with elkhorn coral only inches below the surface. As we neared the island, Tim told me to watch for my gear bag on the beach. In the distance, I spotted a dash of color on the clean sand—my gray gear bag. An airline agent in St. Thomas had found it abandoned in a security cage, radioed our boat about its discovery, and placed it on the local mail boat, which had dropped it at Dead Chest Island. There remained unanswered questions about the logistics—like how did they know that rescued gear bag belonged to a fellow on a boat somewhere in BVI waters? Apparently Captain Tim had been doing some behind-the-scenes follow-up.

I waded ashore and retrieved my gear. I took a moment to look up and down the deserted, pristine beach. "Do you know the story of Dead Chest?" Captain Tim asked. "No? Well, in the days of old, in these parts being a buccaneer was a highly sought-after profession, because they could keep whatever booty they 'salvaged' from the ships they wrecked. Whenever there was room for a new pirate, there were more candidates than positions. Their selection process was simple. They rowed the recruits ashore with the chest containing a single cask of rum. Whoever survived sat on the chest drinking the rum, waiting for the boat to return. Sometimes the bodies of unlucky candidates were dragged to sea to feed the beasts below. The bodies they couldn't find became food for the land crabs. You don't want to wander around the edge of the jungle. You never know whose bones you might stray into."

Losing one's gear might be a poor theme for an anecdote. The ultimate nightmare for a diver is arriving at their dream destination, only to find that their gear did not make it with them. Several lessons unfold. Lesson one: Take as much carry-on as possible. Dive resorts customarily provided a list of recommended carry-on items. On one occasion, my carry-on bag exceeded the allowable limits. I knelt on the airport floor, making split-second decisions about what carry-on items had to go into checked gear. After that experience, my carry-on bag contained only that which could not be replaced or rented. Lesson two: Always find out if the resort carries rental equipment. Lesson three: Adopt a "who cares" attitude and get on "island time" as fast as possible.

While traveling throughout Central America in the 1980s, I accepted that it was foolish to think I could get to the final destination without a glitch. The farther away from civilization I went, the higher the probability of encountering a canceled plane flight, a plane that left early, an airline that had sold my seat to someone else, or a civil war that shut down all air traffic. During one trip, even as a seasoned traveler, I had been the target of a scam and elected to charter a small plane for $1,000 instead of lingering in the local city for the duration of the dive holiday. That story could be a chapter unto itself, but I learned it was always prudent to carry only paid-off credit cards.

In the early 1990s, I looked for a Christmas escape to get away from the commercialism that routinely ransacked my holiday spirit. I booked a last-minute trip to Honduras and took a coworker's dare to travel with a backpack—only a backpack. I fought the urge to stuff it full, and took only the essentials. There was nothing to lose and no gear to fret over. A more liberating experience I have never had.

I adopted the mantra that the journey begins the moment I leave home, not when I arrive at the dive destination, and that made all the tortures of travel more palatable.

CAST AWAY

TRAVEL JOURNAL

Date: June 1986
Location: A nameless Out Island in the Bahamas

Between lost tickets, misplaced gear, and a troubled marriage, I found myself standing alone in a small, ominously quiet airport when I learned my plane had left without me. Stranded again. My bad luck ran around in a frenzy. I took the last remaining seat on an unknown airline to Marsh Harbor, but found myself on a remote island wondering when or if a plane would come for me.

I had just watched the Marsh Harbor runway disappear behind the tail of the plane. This plane should have been down there, not up here. Had there been an unannounced change in flight plans? I sat in the back and could not communicate with the pilot—too many people between him and me. *Relax. Sooner or later I will get to Marsh Harbor.*

We landed. Didn't recognize the island. Didn't even know the direction we were headed. The pilot welcomed us to what sounded like the "hoodlesplats" airstrip and vanished out the window by the pilot's seat. The door beside me opened. Six of us poured out. The others were part of a missionary church group—all very friendly and chatting amongst themselves as they walked off.

I stood by the plane. The pilot looked me over and motioned to where I was supposed to go.

"Customs?" I inquired. An affirmative nod, and we walked toward a small shack.

"Why did we fly over Marsh Harbor?" I said.

The pilot stopped and looked off into space and back at me. "May I please see your ticket."

I tried interpreting his body language—either he forgot or didn't know he had a passenger for a different airstrip. We walked into a small building, where he steered me to customs and immigration, excused himself, and disappeared behind a narrow pea-green door with a crooked sign on it that read "Private." Was he going to fly off and make me someone else's problem? I didn't get the sense that he cared about his wayward passenger. I cleared immigration without taking my eyes off the plane. He was not going to escape out a back window or climb back into that cockpit until there was a plan to get me to Marsh Harbor.

The pilot reappeared. "Come with me." We tossed my gear into the plane. In the air, I watched islands and cays pass by. He descended and made a one-time pass over a small island and swooped in for a landing.

The pilot climbed out his window and opened the passenger door. "Come out and wait over there. Another plane will be here to take you to Marsh Harbor. It should be here soon—only fifteen minutes or so."

I complied.

The pilot saluted casually, revved up the engines, and charged the runway. Soon the sounds of the coral under the wheels faded. Then the sound of the engines diminished. The plane lifted to the skies and banked to the left. The sun lit the top of the wings, making it shine in the deep blue sky. The sea swallowed what was left of the sound of the engine. The plane became a small dot and vanished behind a distant cloud.

It was a signature day with puffy clouds about. Not more than fifty feet to the east was the Atlantic Ocean with a crisp deep blue boasting the promise of clarity. To the west, the Caribbean Sea washed a small beach line with glowing turquoise colors. The far end of the landing strip dead-ended in a patch of scrub bushes. There was no sign of life. And before me, nothing but a crushed coral landing strip that crunched under each step.

I found myself alone. Just me and the sound of the sea and the soft breeze in my ear. I looked around, feeling the warm sun on my head. No hut. No shade. No hat. No water. No food. Just this long strip of crushed coral, a windsock, and me. Where was I?

Fifteen minutes, huh? I looked around to assess my situation and thought how to make the best of the time alone. Looked to my feet. My gray gear bag sat by like an old faithful dog. Been everywhere with me. Here we were—destined to wait. I set the bezel on my watch. Sometimes fifteen minutes feels like an hour.

As the sun rose higher in the sky, it blasted with intensity. My shirt sucked up sweat. I removed it and draped it over my gear bag. Given the circumstances of my unscheduled stop, I wondered if I should worry. Or maybe a better question would have been *when* should I worry?

Five minutes passed. Sweat rolled down the center of my back. The leeward water was luring me in. I stripped and waded in and sat on the sandy bottom.

Where am I?

Fifteen minutes passed. I thought I heard the sound of a distant plane. Wishful thinking? This sense of aloneness began feeling less comfortable. Once I saw a movie where one man in a group of survivors from an airplane crash died as he made his singular trek for help. While the buzzards fed on his remains, the others waited and waited and waited for help that would never come. This was not a good movie to remember. What if…

It was too soon to start thinking about being marooned. I took comfort in the company of my own reflections and turned to the troubling thoughts of what was ahead. But there is something simultaneously cleansing and haunting about being very alone and sitting in the tepid water on an isolated island. Basics, such as food and water, did not enter the survival equation. At least, not yet. In this country, there's a joke about "island time." It's the first culture clash tourists encounter in the Bahamas. "Island time" is the excuse to shrug off why things don't get done. In Mexico it's *"mañana."* Whatever the language or country, it means "It gets done when it gets done." In my case, this meant they could come in fifteen minutes, maybe later, maybe tomorrow. "Relax, mon, we be on 'island time.'"

* * *

Before today, there was actually a plan. I had signed up for a medical research trip in the British Virgins that had happened last week. My itinerary returned me to Miami, and then I was to connect with Dottie on Abaco Island on Saturday, May 31, which was now yesterday. There, we'd spend a week together, trying to sort through the issues that were decomposing the person I loved most in this world.

Weeks before the trip, Dottie decided not to meet me in Abaco. The next day she announced she would. And then it was off again. Her behavior became predictable. First the cancellation, then hours trying to understand her reasoning and working through the issues, and finally, getting her to reverse her decision by agreeing to "sleep on it." These were stressful times. Reasoning with insobriety is madness.

I thought we had the go/no-go decision resolved, but the night before I left for the medical research trip, Dottie canceled once again. I despaired. Did not try to sway her. While driving me to the airport the next morning, Dottie said she would meet me in Abaco, reasoning that not going would probably kill off what shreds were left of our relationship, and this would be a poor way to say goodbye. Despondent, I told her that when I returned Stateside, I would call her at Abaco. If she was there, I would join her. If not, I would head back to Phoenix.

After that, everything went wrong. Everything. While checking in at Phoenix, I was distracted and failed to notice that I gave the agent the wrong destination, and the gear bag got locked up in a St. Thomas security cage. Miraculously, it was recovered a few days ago on Dead Chest Island during the research trip. It vanished again from the British Virgin Islands to Miami and delayed the trip to Abaco a day while I waited for the airline to recover it. In Miami, I handed my ticket packet to the attendant, and the entire packet disappeared. The agent insisted he had returned the tickets. I believed him because I wasn't paying attention and ended up having to purchase a completely new set of tickets. Many months later the airline sent me the recovered tickets. A janitor had found them while cleaning behind the ticket counter. The big lesson is clear: Pay attention at the airline check-in counter, stupid!

Sunday flights to the Bahamas are few but full. Got the last seat on the next flight. It was very expensive, but those who engage in international travel have a tongue-in-cheek joke about flying to developing countries and the Out Islands of the Bahamas group. In those days, the only thing that was predictable was unpredictability. We simply grabbed the next plane headed in that direction. It might work for the adventurous, but it's quite challenging for those who like order and planning. At that time in my life the adventurous part of me grabbed for all the gusto. Even in all this drama, there was something exhilarating about jumping on an airplane without knowing if it would get me to my destination. That's how I'd ended up on this deserted cay.

***

So there I sat—casting my trust to the unknown on this remote island. *Hell, if everything had gone right, I would not have the privilege of sitting in this soothing tepid water on this spit of a landing strip on an unknown island feeling free and admiring all this romantic beauty. So… where is that damned plane?*

I might have been closer to my final destination, but my misadventure was far from over. I did not look forward to having to deal with the troubles with Dottie. Being stuck out here gave me more thinking time.

I drifted into memories of our first visit to Abaco. It was a romantic voyage of carefree times and rejuvenation in the intoxicating lure of island life. I indulged myself in the naïve hope that those times could return. A less optimistic person feared they would not.

Thirty minutes, still no plane.

Maybe I should explore the island and see what was way down there at the other end of the landing strip. Can't be any longer than a mile. That's the standard length of small-plane landing strips in these parts. Should only take an hour up and back. Let's do it.

I swirled around in the water one last time and sat on a rock to dry off. *Should I leave my gear here? What if I go exploring and the plane comes? Maybe it's not such a hot idea after all.*

At last I heard the distant drone of strong engines. I recognized the familiar sound of a DC-3 airplane. My eyes hunted for the source. Maybe it was only a passing plane, not mine. I stood, listening for it to grow or diminish and fade. It was a distant rolling sound, delighting and confusing me at the same time.

My ears followed the sound away from the sunlight as it circled in the distance. Suddenly there was a flicker! Sunlight caught its wing as the plane turned. The growling engine noise grew and drowned out the sound of the sea and breeze. It circled the strip to ensure the runway was clear. My first inclination was to flap my arms like some silly bird, but that wouldn't look cool. Young and vigorous dudes don't flap their arms. But I did breathe a sigh of relief.

The plane came about and aimed for the landing strip. Lower and lower. Lights on. Wheels down. Touchdown! It taxied to the far end and turned.

The door opened. A pilot with big smiling white teeth emerged. "Bet you tot we weren't comin'. Toss me you gear, mon. Come aboard."

I worked my way to the only seat left on the plane—up in the front. Others looked on in curiosity. A woman whispered to her mate, "Who's *that* guy?" One man turned to his companion. "Where are we? What is this place?" Others seemed irritated with the unplanned stopover. Not me.

The plane roared up the coral landing strip and lifted. I looked below to remember the size and shape of this nameless cay. It was truly a deserted island except for this wayfaring landing strip that took people like me and put them momentarily in a twilight zone. Even though my mind had started playing tricks with my aloneness, it had never occurred to me that I could have been in serious trouble. I trusted myself to those entrusted with my care. Sometimes we just need to let go and do that.

About that little island out in the middle of nowhere… Out there in the Bahamas are hundreds of islands—too many to have names or be worthy of space on a map. Over the years I studied avionic charts in search of that landing strip. To this day it remains a mysterious island. If only I had asked the pilot.

Things were different then. I was young with a lust for adventure, and I spent more time taking it all in than worrying about detail. Nowadays I'm not as fast, so planning plays an important role in keeping up with the younger generation. Gotta leverage what you know. When you look at my face, don't let what you see fool you. Inside is still the same kid with that thriving sense of adventure.

DEATH COMES TO THE DREAM

TRAVEL JOURNAL

Date: September 1986
Location: Phoenix, Arizona

My love, my mate on this great voyage—where is she? She vanished without a word. I find myself on a path not of my choosing. How did I get here?

This can't be true. She'll be back. You'll see. This is just a bad dream. Soon I'll wake up and our world will be made whole again. We'll soon sing and dance and frolic in the sun and sand. Yes, tomorrow will be better. You'll see.

But she didn't come back. Not the next day or the day after that. I waited and watched. I left the front porch light on and the door unlocked. But daybreak came, and her side of the bed was cold. I asked my Maker—surely he would explain. *Where is she? Why have you done this to me? I loved for the right reasons. I was faithful and loyal. I treated her well. I followed your path. Why didn't you tell me you were going to take her? Why, Lord, why?*

OK, I get it. There's a lesson in this, right? Tell me what you want, and I'll do it. Whatever it is, I've learned my lesson. I'll do whatever you want. Please, just bring her back to me. Please.

I gazed out the window watching as another cab mistook my driveway for a street. Like all the others, it backed up and went on its way. Moments later I heard the front door open. I hurried down the hall and found Dottie standing in the doorway with her head down. I pulled her into my arms and held her until I was convinced this moment was real. I felt the warmth of her body and her chest expanding with each breath. I was not in a dream. She had come home. We dressed up, went to our favorite restaurant. The place was ours. I played her love songs on the piano. We slipped back into the tepid pool on the August moonlit night. She floated on my fingertips. We made love. She was back. *How can I ever repay you, my Lord? Thank you. Thank you.*

* * *

A few days later I raced home early from work to resume the celebration. Where was she? Nowhere in the house. Nor anywhere outside. Not in the pool. Not in the hammock under the mesquite tree. She had gone for a walk, perhaps. I rocked in my chair, staring at the street through the kitchen window. Waiting. The day sank and the color vanished. The old clock in the hallway sent out a mellow tone. Another hour gone. A passing car sent light that reflected off something out of place on the kitchen counter. I turned on the light, walked over to it, and stood staring into an almost empty bottle of Scotch. How had I missed that? This is what she had left behind? A rage beset me. I grasped the bottle, not understanding the message. I looked up to the ceiling. "No! No! No!" I yelled as I threw the bottle at the wall. It crashed and shattered all over the room. What was left of the amber poison flowed down the wall.

I went outside and stood in the moonlight. I pleaded. I begged. I promised. I wept, and yelled, and whispered. The moon moved halfway across the sky. I was drained, but tears continued to flow. *Please, just tell me if she's coming home.*

In the weeks that followed, I stood at the end of the driveway—waiting for a cab that never came. Neither did answers. I did everything right in that relationship, but the Lord took her anyway. Time did nothing to close the raw wound. My pleading became confusion and anger. The tenets of my beliefs frayed at their edges. Maybe there was no God after all. I gave up. No answers were coming, and all the talk between God and me ended.

THE ROGUE WAVE

TRAVEL JOURNAL

Date: September 1986
Location: Somewhere out in the Sea of Cortez, Baja, Mexico

As the boat headed to port, I waited for others to finish stowing gear to give me more space to sort and pack mine. No sooner had I finished than we noticed a distant breaking wave coming straight at us. Rogue waves sink boats. Could we be the next casualty?

It was the end of a great dive trip. Good weather. Clear water. Calm seas. Good camaraderie. A good escape from the torment of Dottie's recent departure. The afternoon sun beat hard at our backs and on an almost glass-flat sea. The wake from our boat stretched out as the only ripple in the ocean. We plodded along with the same laziness as the summer afternoon. Our lethargy came to an abrupt halt with what we saw coming at us on the water. A single large rogue wave raced toward us with a mind for destruction. We were suddenly very much in harm's way.

When Mother Nature exercises her muscle, she sometimes gives no advance warning. Rogue waves, they call them. I've seen pictures of this phenomena. They're the sea scoundrels that come out of nowhere as they defy wind, current, or any predictable weather pattern. They move quickly with predatory stealth. They are lone large waves hiding behind the darkness of night or coming on the backs of unsuspecting sea captains. They ambush from whichever direction eyes are not turned. They are the sea monsters on the surface that mercilessly wash astern and devour boats. Their name almost implies cunning intelligence.

We scurried to the top deck to study our predicament. We could see the ends of the wave. How odd it seemed—it was heading straight for us. It was a churning, fully flowing cresting wave.

The captain bellowed orders to shut all hatches and prepare ourselves for the plunge. If we kept the bow into it, the wave would pass quickly without harm. But the edges seem to curl around us with a flanking motion. It was assaulting us! The wave grew ominously larger as it approached.

Suddenly we realized what we were facing. It was no rogue wave. We were being treated to a rare privilege from Mother Nature.

We were dumbstruck by their numbers. We estimated that there must have been a thousand of them. Maybe more. Soon they enclosed us. Their energy stirred the water until it developed a surface chop like one from a stiff wind. They leapt everywhere. Some only a few feet away. If my arm were only an inch longer, surely I could have touched them. It was the largest pod of dolphins any of us had ever seen!

What signal did we send that they heard miles away? What language did they speak to universally decide to take time out for frolic? They vied for the underwater bow wake, which to a dolphin is like a wave to surfers. They seemed to have an unspoken agreement to take turns swimming before the boat and leap two or three times completely out of the water before diving deep and giving way to the next "bow rider."

Other dolphins seemed content to race close to the side of the boat, breaching the water in a spectacular demonstration of theatrics. They took delight in coming close and watching us as they jumped into the air for a fresh breath. I scrambled to the lower deck and waved my arms as they appeared. My excitement seemed to encourage them to show off with greater vigor.

They paced us for fifteen minutes, and then with an inaudible signal, they all suddenly turned and resumed their journey northward. The only Kodak moment that existed still lives as a great memory.

I watched as the pod vanished, hoping they would return. The sea returned to its mirror flatness as if nothing had ever happened.

DANCING WITH THE SEA LIONS

DIVE LOG

Date: October 1986
Location: Isla San Pedro Nolasco, Sea of Cortez, Baja, Mexico

The sea lions were particularly playful. They were all over me. Dozens of them shot straight toward me, then turned away moments before contact. They sped within inches of my mask and burped air in my face. As close as they came, they were too fast and agile to be touched.

A NOAA Fisheries booklet advises people not to feed, approach, chase, or otherwise harass sea lions. The booklet also advises to neither attempt to pet nor swim with them. They are wild and unpredictable animals, and people should take all precautions to keep at least eight feet away. The only problem with the advisory is that the memo never got to the sea lions.

I found myself in shallow waters surrounded by at least a dozen of them. I tried mimicking their smooth moves—twisting and turning. They must have been amused with my clumsiness and took turns showing me how to do it properly. The games continued until a territorial bull intervened. His bark needed no translation. It warned, "Get away from my women." When he showed up, his harem scattered in all directions. I was inches away from his face. They are huge—especially when you're right next to them. I have seen how rough things can get when two bulls rumble. Luckily, he saw me as an intruder, not a threat.

My encounter lasted only minutes, yet there was a great honor in our connection. Only rarely do humans have a chance to interact with these highly intelligent beings. The interaction with them gave me a new appreciation for sharing this planet with all creatures.

Back on the boat, I told others of my experience. Lanny, a fellow dive instructor, commented, "It's all in here," as he patted his newfangled gadget, an underwater video camera. The new technology was bulky and unreliable. Sometimes it worked, but mostly Lanny was fussing with it. It did, however, capture the scene with the sea lions. I watched with embarrassment as my ungainly self attempted to show off to the masters of speed and grace. My fellow divers laughed at the scene, yet the sea lions seem to understand the limitations of man far better than man himself.

My encounter with the sea lions was serendipitous. I felt privileged to be among them. I didn't seek them out. We happened to be in the same space in the world. That moment awakened my awareness of why and how they react to humans. And it opened my eyes to the common denominator about how most other creatures receive and interact with humans.

Mother Nature teaches sea life that large things eat smaller things, and humans are larger than most things below. Therefore, humans eat fish. Even to a fish that's basic logic. The less we look like we're on a shopping spree for dinner, the closer we can get to the underwater kingdom. When fish are hungry, they tend to rush in, eat, and run. I found that when photographing fish, I have better luck when I just hang around for ten or fifteen minutes, so they get used to my presence, and then approach slowly from a lower position.

To fish, we look like aliens. That's because we are. The noise from our bubbles is frightful and annoying. The more slowly we exhale, the smaller our bubbles and the less noise we make. And that alone improves our ability to have those close encounters that make diving special.

Sea lions, however, are another story. To them, we are playthings. We are awkward, clumsy. We need masks to see and tanks for air.

Many misinterpret the biblical expression about the "dominion of man" as a measure of intelligence and assume it means we are superior. I doubt if sea lions see it that way. Or orcas. Or octopuses. Or dolphins. Or sea turtles. Or sea otters. Or sharks.

THE FLOWERS OF MIMOSA VILLAGE

TRAVEL JOURNAL

Date: June 1987
Location: Remote village, Roatan, Isla Bahia, Honduras

When the road dead-ended, we walked the rest of the way to the village in search of a legendary and vividly colorful coral-red mimosa tree. We had been told that the villagers were very social, but when one of them ran toward us swinging a machete, it was hard to hold on to the notion that these people were friendlies.

No dive that afternoon. We would rest up for one later that night. But we were rested enough. Six of us decided to find wheels and check out the island. Anthony's Key Resort was a reputable place that gave a good living to the locals and put money into the island community. Visitors announcing themselves as guests from Anthony's Key Resort in any of the villages were quickly treated as dignitaries. The manager threw us keys and gave a few instructions and tips on how to get to the east end of the island where we would find a mimosa tree with fiery red flowers. It was said to be so prolific that mariners and fishermen could see it offshore for miles and used it as a beacon.

The road was narrow and dusty. It followed the contour of the island, hugging ridges and valleys. The uphill roads were washboard—a rippling effect caused by fast cars on dirt surfaces. They rattled our teeth. Anything not bolted down in our van jumped around like sizzling bacon in a frying pan. The road was strewn with shaken-off auto parts. We were warned to use caution while rounding the tops of hills. Oncoming vehicles flew blindly on the wrong side, trying to avoid the washboard effects. Since there were few cars, fast drivers approaching the tops of hills played the odds that no one would be coming the other way.

A tiny village appeared. Dozens of rickety docks extended over the water. All were three feet wide with crooked posts made from tree branches. At the end of each dock was a shack the size of a telephone booth. A storage locker for fishing tackle? Had to check it out. It looked more like an outhouse perched out there than a tackle shack. The docks gave us no confidence in their strength. We tentatively walked down separate docks to visit the mysterious shack on the end. All any of us found inside was a small bench with a hole cut in it. We found ourselves peering into someone's privy. I suddenly felt like an intruder. I wanted to run off that dock before being discovered. It was difficult to understand the ignorance about sanitary conditions. Whatever dropped through the hole fell to the sea below and went wherever it was taken by the tide—back to the beach, down the coast, or out into the ocean currents to feed the world below.

We drove farther and entered French Harbor, the "big city" large enough to support an airport. Peddlers and beggars and would-be thieves lurked in corners and dark places. We scattered to explore and agreed to meet by the town fountain thirty minutes later. Spent my time watching the locals gather in the square—the center of their universe. Women came to launder clothing in a large vat set aside for washing. They were friendly and all chatted at once while conducting a CPR-type rhythmic motion on the clothing against the stone washboard. Two old men sat with their legs crossed on opposite ends of a bench smoking cigarettes and watching the world. No one paid much attention to me. Some glanced. Others smiled. Some greeted me. Mostly they went about their business, accepting this tall stranger in their village.

A medium-sized stake truck approached. It grabbed my eye as it rattled through town. Standing in the bed holding on to the rails were albino black men. They all had Negroid features but skin and curly hair as white as a sheet of paper. My mouth dropped in awe.

I was looking at descendants of the Garifuna, who had been settled there in 1796 by the British. They were originally from St. Vincent in the Lesser Antilles on the eastern side of the Caribbean. They refused to acknowledge European claims to their island when the British won the rights to St. Vincent from France as part of the Treaty of Versailles in 1783. Understandably, they revolted. After nine years, the British grew intolerant of the continuous rebellion and exiled five thousand Garifunas to this island, putting an end to the "problem." I was unsuccessful in learning how this particular group had become white-skinned—later I learned that it was caused by a genetic mutation—except that there were several tribes on the island, and each had unique features that distinguished one tribe from another. Although they were new to me, many of my Central American friends were quite familiar with "los Negros blancos."

Back in the van, we traded stories. Some people boasted of newly purchased mementos. I told of my rare discovery of the white Negroes, and they wondered what I had had to drink.

We resumed our journey to find the legendary mimosa tree. The paved streets of French Harbor ended, and we soon found ourselves back in the quiet jungle on dusty roads. In some places the road hugged the shoreline so closely that it flooded at high tide. Then it abruptly ended. The van could take us no farther.

Through the jungle we could see huts and people. Maybe that was the village with the mimosa tree. We ambled along the beach. Palm trees rustled in the wind. All the huts in the village sat atop stilts and were made completely of palm fronds draped over stick frames. Windows were openings with frond closings propped open with crooked sticks. We could hear children.

Suddenly, off in the distance, a villager stood quickly and pointed at us. They all looked our way and scattered except for the one villager who first spotted us. From our distance, he looked aggravated, and his gestures appeared aggressive. Our jovial mood vanished as we looked around for an exit strategy.

Did we look or act like intruders? The smallest of us towered over these Honduran villagers. We did not know if we should run or brace for combat. We stood dead in our tracks. Silence overwhelmed us as we sorted through our observations.

One villager scurried around and picked up a machete. He began running toward us. This was looking serious. What could we have done so recklessly that it would incense a villager to run at us swinging his machete? He stopped by a small pile of coconuts and picked through them, shaking them close to his ear and throwing them down until he found one that was bright green.

The villager continued his hurried pace—machete poised in one hand and coconut extended in the other. With quick precision, he clipped off the top and drilled a hole in it with his machete.

As he approached, his rush dwindled to a purposeful walk. He stopped ten feet in front of us. The silence was disconcerting. Time stood still. Now what? The machete was still clutched in his right hand but relaxed at his side. I reasoned that once a machete had been taken to a coconut, it was a tool and no longer a weapon.

Our tension melted as a broad smile grew on his dark bronzed face. Lines cut deep into his cheeks as well as around his eyes. He bowed and said something in a tongue we did not recognize. He stepped forward, offering the coconut to one of the men in our group. With raised palms it was refused. "Sorry, I don't like coconut." When offered to the others, it was refused again, and again, and again. It seemed all the villager was trying to do was offer us a coconut. What could be aggressive about that? Each time it was declined, the disappointment on the villager's face became more painful to watch. It was plain he was not just offering a cool drink on a hot day. It was an honorable village ritual. And we were being very rude about it.

My embarrassment grew. His gestures were welcoming, but we were not behaving well. He approached me and tentatively extended the coconut, seemingly fearful of another rejection. His eyes locked on mine. They had the scars of a hard life but were still filled with tenderness and hope. He looked deep into my heart. You can see the soul of a person when you look into their eyes. Eyes tell all. They never lie.

I stepped toward the villager and accepted the coconut. He bowed and took a gentle step backward and once again fixed his eyes deep into mine. I returned the gesture and took a drink. Much to my surprise it was a very sweet tasting flavor. But this was not about coconuts. It was about welcoming visitors to their village. I raised the coconut with both arms, smiled, and bowed once again to my host. It seemed like a good international gesture to express appreciation. It must have been the right one. It brought the broad smile back to his face.

While intimidated by the villager's approach, we had completely overlooked the coral-red mimosa over his shoulder on the other side of the "village square." Knowing these people were not ill-meaning, others in the group excused themselves and walked toward the tree. I stayed put, giving full attention to the villager who stood alone with me mumbling something incomprehensible but in a gentle, humble voice. The tree with red flowers became trivial.

Soon more villagers appeared. Others handed me coconuts with cut-off tops. I juggled three and sampled them all. Children surrounded me while touching my arms and tugging at my shirt. What had I done?

Villagers must know their coconuts. How did my greeter know to pick out the one he did? My first taste of coconut was back in grade school when a student brought one to class for a "show and tell" activity. What I tasted then was bitter, and it left me with an inflexible resolve to never sip coconut water again. I thought about how this man had picked up several coconuts, shaken them, listened, and felt them until he had the right one. Later, my research removed much of the mystery. Here's some coconut lore. It has no direct bearing on this story, but there will be a test at the end.

> Coconuts go through four phases. Phase one and two coconuts are almost identical in their green color. They differ in the water content within. During phase one, the coconut water is white, rich, and sweet. As the coconut matures, the fat separates from the water and clings to the wall of the nut and diminishes the water content. An expert can tell which phase the coconut is in by the feel and the sound of the water.
>
> Phase two coconut water takes on a bitter taste and is unacceptable for welcoming visitors.
>
> Phase three occurs when the white paste inside the nut hardens as the water all but vanishes inside. The coconut becomes dry, brittle, and hard to open. Want delicious high fat and high cholesterol coconut meat? Grab yourself a phase three coconut. This is the coconut phase found in grocery stores.
>
> Phase four is the miracle. That's when a leaf pops out of one end and a root foot comes out the other, and life begins again. It's considered a miracle because the leaf always pops out the end that's up.
>
> Then there are amber-yellow coconuts. They are the drones. I have seen them used for soccer. All of the coconut and palm trees are put to good use for building materials, firewood, and canoes, among other things.
>
> So… pop quiz… If you were a villager seeking the perfect coconut to offer a visitor, how would you know what to select?

Now you know all I know about coconuts. Enough coconut lore.

We stood in awe as we basked in the coral redness of the mimosa tree. It was not as tall as we'd expected, but it had a thick, broad canopy with sprawling limbs. This tree, some villagers told us, was constantly dropping and sprouting new blossoms. The brilliant colors not only filled the tree itself, but blanketed the ground below.

While talking with another villager, I learned of a mountain road over the island that would cut an hour off our return trip. We decided to take it, as the day was beginning to fade and the incoming tide would submerge the road that had brought us to this faraway village. I had nothing to give my new friend—the man with the coconut—for his hospitality. We clasped hands and looked again into each other's soul. That was goodbye enough.

The road over the mountain began to be not such a good idea. It grew steep and narrow. We were in Honduras, which is a Spanish word that describes mountains that plunge abruptly from the sky into the ocean. They are not steep as in hard to climb; some can be scaled only with ropes—as in rappelling. If a vehicle went over the edge, the fast-growing jungle foliage would quickly conceal the evidence and those poor souls at the bottom of the barrancas would never be found. The road defined the ridge. It became more like a pathway than a road. Erosion and cuts tested our mettle to continue. There was no safe place to turn around without anxiety, furious arm waving, and a lot of yelling of conflicting orders from the armchair generals in the van. Choices were few as our nervousness increased.

We found ourselves head-to-head with a Honduran farmer leading a donkey with large bunches of bananas tied to its back. One of us had to give way. I got out of the van and approached the rugged-looking Honduran.

"Esta todo bien con este calle?" [Is the road OK?]

"Calle?" He smiled as he questioned my calling this pathway a "road." But, yes, it was clear to the other side. As we headed down the ridge, it occurred to me that what may have been a good donkey road was looking impassable for a van.

As quickly as we vanished into the jungle, we found ourselves at a crossroads with the same dirt road with the washboard hills that had shaken our teeth only a few hours before.

Later, when relating our adventure to the hotel manager, I learned it was a custom to offer a freshly cut coconut to approaching visitors as they entered the village. Our hosts had been upset about their own rudeness for not noticing us sooner, until we were well within village limits. The villagers who scattered weren't scurrying for weapons. Instead, they had hustled out to gather children for the welcoming party. Imagine how they had felt when we refused their hospitality.

As a traveler, I was becoming more culturally aware. We fear those who look, talk, or live differently. A man ran at us swinging a machete. I thought "threat," whereas the villagers were embarrassed about their seeming lack of hospitality. My culture can impede understanding the culture of others. From looking into that villager's eyes, I knew they placed high value on community, hospitality, and tradition. That day, while searching for the flowers of Mimosa Village, I discovered that human kindness is first found in the eyes of our hosts, and when understanding other cultures—look for goodness and sameness. And when language fails, good communication begins. That is, if we have the vision to see past our blindness.

PADRE FELIPE

TRAVEL JOURNAL

Date: June 1987
Location: San Pedro Sula, Honduras

I stood gazing out the airport window waiting for my plane. I could hear nothing. No thoughts bounced around my head. No one was waiting for me back home. There was really no place to go but "back there." I had no God. I had no mate. I was empty. What was happening to me? What path was I on?

Padre Felipe was a Jesuit priest assigned to Honduras in the early 1940s for missionary work. His legacy was setting up Christian radio throughout Central America. After World War II, he purchased the radio tower on Guadalcanal after it was classified as "army surplus." He traveled to the Solomon Islands, climbed the tower, mapped out each piece, disassembled it, packed it, and had it shipped to Honduras, where he hired a local for twenty dollars to reassemble it. He spent decades traveling throughout Central America setting up and teaching the locals how to use his radio network and using it for his missionary work.

After a dive trip to Roatan, Honduras, I sat relating tales of traveling to Honduras to Mom. She told me I should go find Padre Felipe. He was family, Mom's cousin, and had been in Central America for almost half a century.

I lost track of the number of times I arrived in Central America looking for Padre Felipe only to discover he had "just left" for another country. He'll return in a month or so, they said.

Finding Padre Felipe became my quest. Can't say why or what drove me. Perhaps it was the story Mom told about his paddling a canoe through the rivers of the United States to get to the seminary in New York. Or it was the picture of a young priest, somewhere in Central America, sitting in a wooden cart being pulled by a donkey. Maybe it was an admiration for a man who followed his calling and his dream, no matter where it took him. I just knew I had to find this man.

Padre Felipe was the catalyst for learning Spanish well enough to venture hundreds of miles away from anyone who could speak English. I went in and out of countries the US State Department said were dangerous—unrest, civil war, coups, and thieves dropping out of the jungles to stop passing cars in the mountain regions. I dressed like locals, learned their cultures, ate their food, sat among them on hot lazy afternoons in the village squares, and let the sun darken me up. Blending in became easy. I let my guard down, believing I had become accepted. Imagine my exhilaration on the day when a Honduran family stopped me in an airport and asked for directions.

Was I searching for Padre Felipe or was I actually pursuing something else, or trying to become someone I wasn't and could never be? Was I merely fleeing?

Many immigrants send money back to their families in Central America. I read articles about how the mail had been intercepted and torn apart by people looking for money or checks. When I began using that old-fashioned see-through-the-envelope paper, more of my correspondence reached Padre Felipe. The mail system was predictably slow—anywhere from two weeks to months.

> Dear Padre Felipe,
> I plan on being in Honduras on [this date]. I will be passing through San Pedro Sula on my way to Isla Bahia. Below is my flight information. I know the drive from the mountains in Yoro takes four hours and is very tiring, but if you're in the country, it would be good to connect with you. I will keep an eye open for you.
> Sincerely yours,

Many of my letters must not have reached Padre Felipe. I came and went, year after year, standing in airport waiting rooms scanning for a person without a description. Maybe someone was there looking around for me.

Another year and another opportunity at the San Pedro Sula airport. I spotted a man standing in the center of the waiting room. He was elderly, partially stooped over, and had a thin face with a square jaw and wire-rimmed glasses. He was easily a head taller than anyone else in the room. Could it be? I stepped up to him. We looked at each other.

"Jeff?" said the man.

I grabbed my gear and tossed it into his jeep, and off we drove to a neighboring town, Progresso, where he had his beginnings in Central America.

"When do you have to be back for your flight?"

"We have about six hours."

"Are you hungry?"

"Always."

"Where would you like to go?"

I spotted a Pizza Hut. "Do you like pizza?"

"I have never had it."

"Well, then, you're in for a treat."

We sat looking over the menu. "See anything you like?"

"Why don't you pick something for me."

I ordered safely: a large veggie pizza with extra cheese.

Padre Felipe took one bite and his eyes lit up. "This *is* good!"

After eating two slices, he closed the box, covering 60 percent of what was left. "Don't you want more?" I asked.

"I want all of it, but I want to take this back to the village in Yoro and share it with the nuns in the kitchen at the mission."

In all my pizza-eating days, the best pizza I had ever eaten to that point was in the Pizza Hut in Progresso, Honduras.

We sat talking, catching up on all the years I had missed him, his beginnings in Central America, how he had established the radio network, and how some of my adventures placed me in peril as I freely traveled around Central America during a time of major civil wars and communist revolutions. He lamented I didn't have more time, because he wanted to take me to his mission in Yoro. We agreed that the next time I came to Honduras, I would visit his mountain. We talked of spending a week or two in the northern regions exploring the Mayan ruins, a mere four-hour drive away.

"All those years you have been here… Are you glad you came?" I asked him.

"When I joined the seminary, I told them I wanted to be assigned to Central America. I arrived without knowing a word of Spanish, and the government was never stable in those days. I came here to teach, but I learned more from the people than they could have learned from me."

"What was that?"

"They taught me how to be happy with nothing. They have nothing. Those who were born in poverty live and die in poverty. There is no opportunity for advancement. They are happy when their bellies are full. Fifty percent of babies die at birth while the parents celebrate their blessings with the half who live. Their values are found in their families, their communities, being kind and generous with one another. No one has closets filled with clothing. What they wear is all they own. They accept disaster and death and life as gifts from God. They trust all people until those people prove to be untrustworthy. That was the way of things around here back when I first arrived in the early forties. Much has changed, but those basic simple values have survived the generations. This is more of a home than where I came from. I don't know if I could ever go back."

"Maybe you can help me," I said.

"With what?"

"God and I are not on speaking terms."

Padre Felipe sat back, smiled, and looked away pensively. "I am not one to make a judgment, but I have never known God to not want to talk to his people. He's always listening. It's up to you to say something, and you will in good time. Come. It's getting late, and soon I will have to get you back to the airport, but first, I want to show you where I first came when I arrived as a young Jesuit priest."

Although it had been years since he had been assigned to the mission in Progresso, he remained welcomed and revered. The pizza didn't make it to Yoro as planned. Instead, Padre Felipe gave it to the nuns in the kitchen in Progresso, who all giggled with excitement over this "comida extraño" [new kind of food].

We walked down a corridor and stopped by a framed photograph on the wall. "See this picture?" He pointed to a face in a group photo. "That's me." Then he pointed to about twelve others, his finger stopped on each, saying, "He was killed" or "She was killed."

"Wow! What happened?"

"Years ago, during one of the insurrections, guerillas stormed the mission and killed them all—nuns and priests alike. Before killing the nuns, they dragged them naked through the streets. Some were raped, but all were murdered in the town square, where they forced the villagers to watch. They told them the killings were on their shoulders. The mission of the Order is to teach, and knowledge is the enemy of insurrectionists. If the people hadn't gone to the mission to learn, none of the nuns or priests would have been killed."

"But how did you survive it?"

"I had left the country the day before to take care of radio business. Come, let me show you the radio tower from Guadalcanal that I purchased from the US government after it was decommissioned."

Padre Felipe was a humble man. He would answer questions about his past but was not one to dwell on anything that might bring praise for his life's work.

Padre Felipe drove me to the airport. We said our goodbyes amidst promises of reconnection. I had a feeling that I might never see him again.

* * *

Even though our marriage had ended, Dottie's passing left a big hole. I wept bitterly at the loss but was thankful that in death she had found peace and freedom from the torments of alcohol. I could never forgive myself for forcing her to choose between the bottle and me, and those who cannot forgive themselves walk a dark path littered with a sense of betrayal. I lost perspective. I lost touch with my own feelings, and in doing so, I lost touch with others. Without empathy, I had become just… empty.

I sent a letter off to Padre Felipe. I described my disdain for my inner self and that I thought immersion in the Central American culture could realign my moral compass and give me a renewed sense of purpose. I offered my skills in the building trades in exchange for a roof over my head and food. I offered to work in the fields and be servants of farmworkers, bringing them food and water. I pleaded. I had convinced myself that living among them for a month or two would free me from the chains of my guilt. Maybe being in God's house would pry open the door and I could once again speak to Him.

Months passed. One day a small package arrived containing my opened letter and a response from someone in Yoro, Honduras. Padre Felipe had returned to the States due to failing health. They thought he had gone to Texas to be with his sister. In my effort to contact her, I came across her obituary. To me, Padre Felipe was lost.

Through him, I developed a deep appreciation and respect for the Central American people. They embodied the values that mattered—kindness, family, acceptance, forgiveness, generosity. I wanted to be accepted by them. I wanted to be one of them.

I could never explain my near obsession with connecting with Padre Felipe. His influence on me was great long before I ever met him. The few hours we spent in Progresso became a memory that would never lose its freshness.

Years later, in 2012, I renewed my search for Padre Felipe and found his obituary in a St. Louis, Missouri, funeral announcement. He had died three years earlier. At first I was sad that I had not known. But then again, how could anyone have known about the relationship between Padre Felipe and me? And, with the knowledge of his passing, I was the only one left in this world who could bear witness to our friendship.

We are all blessed with stories like mine. We are told that we should not live in the past, but visiting an old memory to brush aside the dust of time is among the great strawberries in our lives.

FRANCES THE NURSE

TRAVEL JOURNAL

Date: July 1987
Location: The highway to San Carlos, Mexico

After driving with her for an hour, I began crafting nefarious plans to ditch this nonstop babble mouth at the next wide spot on this desolate highway.

"I hear you're planning to drive to Mexico," said Bronx. "Frances is riding with you. She drives me crazy. All she does is talk, talk, talk. I don't want her in my truck. Period. I'll tell her I have no room and you need the company."

That was my introduction to Frances. She was a big-boned blond woman with wild hair. Her large blue eyes focused with intensity. She talked relentlessly. I quickly understood why she had been handed over to me. As anecdotes popped into her head, she flew off with animation and excitement about something from yesteryear. There was no connection between one tale and the next. To Frances, listening to nothing but road noise was taboo—air had to be filled with talk. We were driving through the flat, arid deserts of Mexico with blue-gray mountains lining the horizon. Occasionally we passed a tall cactus plant shriveling from dehydration. Frances watched the landscape, pointed, and burst out with "Look! That reminds me of a story." I could see nothing in the landscape that would trigger her imagination. How could a person talk so much?? Was her talking an addiction? Was she lonely and had no one to talk to at home? Was she trying to find herself in her stories? I smiled and nodded in respect, but all that did was encourage her.

The journey between Phoenix and San Carlos, Mexico, was normally an excruciating eight hours with or without company. With Frances as my travel mate, however, time passed quickly, even though she was a blabbermouth. She was a storybook on tape. She was a radio that could not be turned off. She talked about travel, customs around the world, and problems in other countries and in the United States, and she stared off into space, endlessly wondering and speculating about why people behave as they do. When I looked into her eyes and saw her zest for life, I began to see the person of yesterday in the person sharing the front seat of my truck. With all her jabbering and wandering, Frances had something to say, and I found it was worth listening to her.

When Frances needed a talking break, she whacked me on the arm. "So, what's your story?" My stories never reached completion. Actually, they never got started. She constantly interrupted with questions about missing details that took us down lost trails on never-to-return tangents. Tangents became the doorway to more tangents, and whatever "my story" was became foreign even to me. Soon Frances tired of the drifting and retreated to her own stories. It was her unquenchable curiosity that drove her line of questions, and I discovered things about myself that had lain hidden by my lack of curiosity for years. Frances taught me the magic of asking questions when listening to others. "Asking questions makes you a good listener," asserted Frances. After she asked "why" half a dozen times, I found myself standing in the middle of real meaning.

Frances was an army nurse during World War II. Nurses were well respected. Men were quick to fall in love with them. They feared dying on the battlefield without a loved one back home waiting for them. Frances found herself engaged to three servicemen at the same time. She kept white medical tape wrapped around each ring with the name of its giver—just to be sure she wore the right one with the right man on liberty. In the end, she married someone else altogether. None of her beaus died in action. None returned for their rings.

When asked how she could have been in love with three men at the same time, she flailed her arms as she explained. "First you have to understand that the ideals, culture, and values in the forties were more uniform than those here in the eighties, and almost any man would make a good husband. Back then, values and beliefs were less diverse, and marriage was less risky than it is now. This may sound corny, but a gal could pick a man she thought handsome, and she'd still be marrying someone with good values. These days, if a woman married for looks, it would be a crapshoot that the marriage could work at all." Frances gazed out the window as if looking into the past. "The old days were better."

Scuba diving was not something Frances simply wanted to do so she could cross it off the things-to-do list before dying. She had zest, passion, and a never-ending curiosity. She was a fascinating woman and an attentive dive buddy. You see, Frances was seventy years old and still in love with life. And, as a nurse, she had served under Erwin Rommel. You know, the Desert Fox—that formidable German commander who, under Adolf Hitler, confounded his enemies in Africa between 1940 and 1942.

Frances was affable. So she was a tad loquacious. Sometimes we all get overly talkative. During that dive weekend, when I quit being annoyed with her, I found her to be a delight. After that one trip, I never saw her again. I wonder whatever became of Frances, my truck mate to San Carlos, Mexico.

ANCHOR'S AWAY

DIVE LOG

Date: July 1987
Location: Lighthouse Cove, Isla San Pedro Nolasco, Mexico

The line broke in the strong winds and left our anchor on the ocean floor. If we could not recover it, our trip was over. Retrieving it in the rough seas would be perilous without the proper lift equipment.

This was a big weekend for me. It was my divemaster certification checkout. Our plan included driving from Phoenix to San Carlos, Mexico, and heading out on a three-hour boat ride to a small far-offshore island named San Pedro Nolasco.

Six of us met at the Aqua Sports dive shop in Phoenix at 4:00 a.m. Bronx locked the store and walked over to the group. "OK, guys. This trip is Jeff's divemaster evaluation. He will be your divemaster. He's had a lot of experience with us, and I can assure you that he is as competent as any divemaster out there. From here on, it's his call."

I looked to the east and then to the group. "Good morning. Well, almost good morning. There's a tiny band of light in the east, so I guess that counts as morning. We have an eight- to nine-hour trip ahead of us, and when we cross into Mexico, we'll have to go through immigration. They'll be asking for ID, and we've already told you to bring your passport or driver's license. Before we head out, let's do a check. Please show me your identification. If we get to the border and you don't have it, you'll be sitting there until we come back Sunday night."

Everyone presented their license or passport except Todd. He stood looking at me. "Could you please show me your ID, Todd?"

"I have it. Don't worry."

"I'm sure you do. May I please see it?"

"I said I have it. I don't need to be treated like some first grader."

"I'm sorry you feel that way. We just don't want to leave you at the border. Please show it to me or I'm afraid you won't be going with us."

"You're telling me that you're not going to allow me to go unless I show you identification? I can't believe this. This is no way to treat a paying customer."

"I'm sorry, Todd, but this is the way it has to be. It's for your protection."

Todd looked away in disgust and felt for his wallet. "I didn't bring my driver's license. Since I wasn't going to drive, I figured there was no sense in it."

"No problem. Just show me your passport."

Todd rummaged through his backpack. "It's not here. I must have left it on the kitchen table."

We made a side trip to Todd's home. He offered no apologies. His arrogance overshadowed any evidence of humility. No lessons learned here. Not a good sign.

We arrived in San Carlos by midafternoon. At the marina, we stood dockside next to our dive boat, *Bravo*. I assembled the divers for a short briefing on boat orientation, safety, where to stow or not stow gear, and what they could expect on our crossing to San Pedro Nolasco Island. The divers settled in, and I spent my time practicing Spanish with Captain Vicente and the mate.

San Pedro Island was a steep granite monolith protruding from the blue-black depths of the Sea of Cortez. Above the waterline, it was almost pure white with pelican poop. Infrequent rain left the white poop so thick that from a distance it looked like ice cream topping on a cake.

Typical anchorage consisted of setting the bow anchor in deeper water, backing within twenty feet of the island, and casting a small stern anchor to the cliffs to hook a rock at the waterline. The stern anchor kept the boat from drifting or swaying on the bow anchor. Even when only a few feet from the rocks, the boat sat in ten to fifteen feet of water.

It was our practice to treat all certified divers as competent individuals. Boat crew assisted in tank attachment and helped divers into their gear. It was the diver's responsibility to monitor their depth and bottom time, and to perform all dive table calculations before jumping in.

While divers were down, I kept a vigilant watch, "reading" the exhaled bubbles to identify each diver and studying them for potential problems below. I sat on the upper deck of the boat, dreading the thought that Bronx would appear and present me with a pop quiz about "who was where."

Todd geared up a little too soon for his next dive. I questioned his surface interval, thinking there may have been a miscalculation with his dive tables. He assured me his math was good and proceeded with dive preparation. I consulted with Bronx. She advised me to ask him for his dive planning worksheet.

"I thought you told us we were responsible for ourselves. Why should I show you my math for the next dive?" Todd became aggravated with my persistence but handed me his worksheet.

"Todd, there's a math error here. On your last dive you stayed down longer than you should have, and technically, you're bent."

"Well, as you can see, I'm not." Todd snatched the paper back to double-check his work. I went to Bronx for coaching and was told to stand my ground. If Todd developed the bends, there could be a lawsuit even though it was his fault.

"Todd, can we talk on the bow, please."

"Why can't we talk here? I have nothing to hide from the others. Besides, I want them to hear what you have to say."

"Please... join me at the bow."

Reluctantly, Todd followed me forward.

"Todd, you blew the tables. It happens. I can see how easy it is to make a math error. We can't allow you to go back in."

"So I have to sit it out? How long?"

"You have to stay out for twenty-four hours to clear the tables."

"What! Are you serious? The dive trip will be over by then."

"I know you learned the dive tables and what you have to do if you blow them. You have to sit it out. You know this. There's no getting around it."

Todd became argumentative and demanded we return his money. He resorted to name-calling and bad language. He made others uncomfortable, including me. It would have been up to me to contain any outbreaks. Thought I'd let him settle down. Acting too soon would be like throwing gasoline on a fire. Minutes later he retreated to the bow to mend his ego.

I had never seen such belligerence from a diver before. Why did it have to happen during my evaluation trip? Something about him had bothered me from the beginning.

The rest of the day was uneventful. I spent the afternoon in an underwater mapping exercise at Lighthouse Cove. This was a sedate location with plenty of wind protection, and it was a good place for anchorage and night diving. I plotted the location of rocks and what the terrain looked like near the island's edge. I even found a discarded stove.

Some divers prepared for the night dive. Time for a briefing. With great authority from my mapmaking exercise, I told them about the bottom contour, the location of the old stove, and where to find prolific cup coral that would be open and fiery orange in color. It was during the briefing that the value of underwater mapping became clear, and maps have become a permanent part of my logs and journals.

When all my chickens were home, I readied my bedding. It did not take long to drift off.

Something woke me with a start. I sat up straight and looked to my left. The rocky island seemed close. We were only a few feet from it. The anchor must have been dragging in the stiff winds. I sprang to my feet. My voice pierced the night wind as I called sharply for Captain Vicente. In an instant he was up. With a flick of the wrist, he untied the stern anchor line and flung it overboard. I tended to the bow anchor line to take up the slack but encountered no resistance. The anchor was gone. The engine howled as we escaped just a few blinks from slamming into the rocks.

We inspected the end of the rope. There was no fray, and the loop that attached it to the anchor chain remained intact. We concluded that the bolt holding the anchor rope to the chain had either broken or come loose. It could have worked itself out in all the tugging in the wind. Vicente usually had it wired to the chain so it could not unscrew, and he was too competent a captain to overlook that important detail. I suspected foul play but kept it to myself. We had a problem to solve.

Lighthouse Cove had always been a safe harbor. When *Bravo* was out of harm's way, Bronx, Vicente, and I discussed our options. The night was pitch black, and the treacherous seas wiped out visibility. A nocturnal recovery of the anchor was not an option.

We moved to North Point, the lee side, where we would attempt to use the sand anchor. Given the one-hundred-foot depth, we needed seven hundred feet of anchor scope to ensure a good bite, yet all we had was three hundred feet, and that was insufficient for a reliable set. It would have to do. The only remaining option was to head back to San Carlos in a stiff wind and heavy head seas.

We assigned ourselves to night-watch. I took the first shift. Staying awake was difficult. Vicente came on deck and went to the bow. He tested the anchor rope with his foot, said it was holding tight, suspended the watch duty, and returned to his bunk. He had more confidence in the anchor's bite than me. He was the captain, and I trusted his judgment, but I leaned against the wheelhouse and vowed to stay awake… just in case.

We were well sheltered at North Point. Wind would not cause anchor drag. A strong tidal current, however, could give us trouble, but Vicente said it would hold. If I nodded off, it would not be dereliction of duty.

Hours later, at first light, I woke up to find us adrift. The anchor had pulled loose, and now it was just hanging straight down into the abyss. The bottom was over a thousand feet below. Later I chuckled at the picture I drew in my logbook of the anchor hanging down, hoping to snag some passing pinnacle.

San Pedro Nolasco was far off to the west. We must have been adrift for hours. Vicente appeared. Asked me what I had done with the island. Started the engine, pulled up the dangling anchor, and headed toward the island for breakfast.

The wind was not our friend that morning. North Point was our only lee on the island, and the sand anchor was ineffective. We assessed the situation in Lighthouse Cove and decided to retrieve the anchor, knowing conditions would deteriorate as the morning aged. This was our best chance. We decided to go for it. The *Bravo* pitched and yawed. The dive platform slapped at the water like a flyswatter.

Bronx and I discussed the plan, donned gear, climbed onto the back platform, stepped into the froth, and vanished below. We dropped to the bottom, making a zigzag search pattern. Finding the anchor so quickly was a credit to Vicente's knowledge of these waters. Visibility was low and worsening by the minute. Bronx tended to the anchor, and I followed the anchor chain, searching for the all-important bolt needed to fasten the anchor chain to the rope. Send me medals! I found it! Boy! Was I ever going to be a hero, finding this two-inch-long bolt in all this murk!

Bronx prepared to surface with the anchor, using her BC as a lift bag. This was risky and potentially dangerous, but we had no real lift bag. The anchor was forty or fifty pounds. It would take all the air her BC could hold to lift the anchor, even with kicking. If Bronx let go, she would shoot uncontrollably to the surface and risk an air embolism. Or, if she became entangled and it fell back to the bottom, it would pull her down so quickly, it could cause serious ear injury. But if we were going to retrieve the anchor, this was the most expeditious way under the severe conditions. Bronx was a master instructor and safe with her students to a fault, but when it came to her own personal safety, she sometimes sidestepped the rules.

I assigned myself as tender to help control our ascent. We gave each other a nod and slowly began the dangerous journey to the surface.

As we ascended to shallow water, we could feel the force of the wave action. We were suddenly sucked to the surface, but the anchor remained secure as Bronx kept a sharp focus on her task. Vicente maneuvered the boat next to us, and the mate grabbed the anchor.

The next tricky task was retrieving the stern line.

We descended and headed toward the rocks where Vicente had cast the stern line free the night before. The visibility worsened, and the surge grew more forceful as we went shallow. Maintaining control became impossible. We found ourselves at the mercy of the surge— that strong flow of water in one direction, then the other. Surge is what causes sea fans to sway back and forth in those alluring underwater films we see.

We found the loose end of the stern line. We waited for a momentary lull in the surge, and Bronx vanished behind a boulder to free the anchor that was firmly grasping the shoreline rocks. She was gone a long time. The surge cycle strengthened, trapping her in a bad place. I fruitlessly attempted to fasten myself to a rock to withstand the surge, but it ripped and sloshed, preventing a good grip. Where was Bronx?

I thought about surfacing to look for her bubbles—or maybe Bronx herself. It would be more dangerous up there than where we were. I was growing increasingly anxious. The surge cycle let up. Now was a good time to surface and search for bubbles. As I readied myself, Bronx appeared from around the boulder, beat up but doing well and with the small stern anchor in her arms.

The line fouled around us, intertwining us in it. Bronx attempted to untangle us. The surge increased again and swept her toward a sharp boulder. I lunged toward her and buffeted her collision. The surge then swept us back out. We worked our way into deeper, safer water.

Back on the surface, conditions had grown uglier and rougher while we were down. The mate yelled, "Cuidado! Que fao, el mar," warning us to be careful with the "ugly sea." He took the stern line and anchor.

The boat ladder stabbed at the water like an insane maniac. The platform continued to slap hard at the water. "How the hell are we going to get up that?"

"When you grab hold of the ladder," yelled Bronx, "do not let go of it under any circumstances! I'll go first. You watch."

She approached the boat and waited for the sea to settle. It would not cooperate. Vicente maneuvered masterfully as he kept the sea from bullying his ten-ton piece of floating iron. Bronx timed her approach, and when the ladder stabbed deep into the water, she quickly grabbed it and hooked her fins on the bottom rung. The stern rose high, then dipped deep under water. Bronx held on tight—washed like a golf ball in one of those red cleaning cans at the tee box.

It was my turn. No more instructions. Just go. No lingering. I grabbed the ladder, attached myself firmly to it, and got the same wild bull ride I had watched Bronx take.

This dive was one of many encounters with the rages of the sea. Bronx and I made good dive buddies. She was neither docile nor reckless. She was always a dive professional, but she liked it electrifying. Sometimes we experienced situations that stress-tested the buddy system. I quit counting the number of underwater buddy assists I made to untangle or unwedge her in her quest to spearfish our next meal. When back on the boat, she looked and gave me an acknowledging nod, and that was the extent of discussion. It was her way of thanking me. Bronx and I respected each other's dive skills even though she was once my instructor. Although we never spoke of it, our bonds grew out of trust.

In 2015, I stood across the street from Aqua Sports, once the most highly esteemed dive shop in Phoenix. All that remained was a dilapidated row of unidentified stores and boarded-up windows as its rotting carcass sat below a tall billboard, waiting for someone to buy the property, raze the building, and erase whatever was left of that part of diving history.

Such a moment struck a chord, reminding me that nothing is forever, and we should savor all we can while we can. In recalling that weekend on San Pedro, I wondered if disgruntled Todd had had something to do with the mysterious unbolting of the anchor while he was licking his wounds on the bow. If he did have a hand in it, then I have to thank him for one of the most exhilarating of more than three dozen dive trips I made to San Carlos, Mexico.

LOST IN THE DARK

DIVE LOG

Date: September 1987
Location: Carmen Island, Baja, Mexico

I'll never be the designated dive buddy again.

Mark and Rita were cocky, arrogant divers, but they were nervous about jumping into the water on this, their first night dive. Like a big brother having to drag his kid sister to the ballpark, I was the designated driver on the dive. Gave Mark and Rita instructions on dive lights etiquette, like not blinding each other by shining it directly into each other's eyes or waving it wildly—a distress signal—to get someone's attention to see a cleaner shrimp's antenna sticking out from under a rock. I dealt with the nervousness most first-time night divers face and knew it would diminish once they were down. There is a powerful peace found in night diving. Once down, they were immediately at home.

I took the lead, but when I looked back to check on them, they were gone. Among my greatest fears in diving is losing a buddy. My heart raced. I looked around. No lights. No divers. Looked to the surface. Not there. They were my responsibility, and I had lost them. Turned off my light, searching for lamp glow. Relieved, I caught glimpse of a faint light reflected seconds before they ventured too far. They swam around the point—off-limits on night dives, since their bubbles and underwater lights cannot be monitored if land comes between the watchful divemaster on the boat and a down diver.

I caught up with them and grabbed Mark's fin to get his attention. He turned and gave me a *What's your problem?* look. In return, I gave him my angry divemaster glare, but my face was not visible. How I wanted to shake a scolding finger at them. Once back on the boat, however, I would have to report the incident and turn the disciplinary action over to the head divemaster. I hate being around know-it-all divers.

I turned my light off again. The moon lit up the water and created definition with the underwater landscape, casting a glow about the entire ocean. My breathing slowed, and I felt comforted with my weightlessness and the guiding light from my dear friend the moon. My anger with my new night divers became insignificant.

Up to now I had brought airplane landing light candlepower with two or three small backup lights on night dives. This was my first time to dive without lights, and it was after that dive that I began spending my night dives swimming in the dark, seeing beyond the light and what the light could not show.

Back on the boat, I did not take Mark and Rita to the bow for "a word." I figured it would do no good. Arrogance causes deafness, and it ain't worth talking if you won't be heard. Besides, they introduced me to diving with lights out, not a bad trade.

MY DEEPEST DIVE

DIVE LOG

Date: November 1987
Location: Isla San Pedro Nolasco, Mexico

We descended headfirst down the anchor line to the bottom, 125 feet below. No time to waste, with maximum bottom time of fifteen minutes. Because we made a rapid descent, nitrogen narcosis hit me hard. The last I saw of John was his fins vanishing in the darkening deep water. I had to stop him but knew going after him would make this a forbidden decompression dive.

Six of us divemasters from the shop headed to Mexico for a weekend of diving without students, customers, or responsibility for anyone except ourselves. We could solo dive, buddy dive, or not dive. The freedom was ours to do as we wished.

There was talk of hammerhead sharks seen at North Point in deep water. We knew the site well, but our fifteen-minute maximum bottom time included time for descending, visiting, ascending, and a three-minute safety stop. We knelt on a ledge at 125 feet surrounded by a field of black coral. Their polyps glowed and looked as if a winter storm had left them covered in snow. The constant snapping of shrimp claws disappeared sixty feet above. Breathing air felt like sucking syrup, and our exhaust bubbles crackled like shattering crystal. I felt like I had drunk three martinis on an empty stomach. Focusing was almost impossible.

A shadow of something approached. I strained hard through the narcosis to make out its shape. It appeared as an oozing cloud of darkness.

Could it be hammerhead sharks? John signaled that he wanted to investigate, but it meant going deeper. I pointed to my depth gauge and wagged my finger: *No*. John motioned for me to stay at that level while he went deeper to investigate. Stupefied with narcosis, I nodded. John vanished. The other buddy teams headed back to the surface.

What kind of a buddy am I?? I shook off the narcosis and kicked hard to catch up to him. At 145 feet I snagged his fin moments before he plunged off a ledge into dangerously deep water. He stopped and looked at me, and without hesitation we headed back to the anchor line. This occurred before the advent of dive computers, so we had effectively "blown the tables." By retrieving John from the deep, we both had passed the limits of recreational sport diving. We had now been down too deep for too long. If we ascended directly to the surface, we were almost assured that decompression sickness would kill or paralyze us for life.

We ascended slowly. At eighty feet, my narcosis dwindled, and clear thinking returned. Our normal optional three-minute safety stop at fifteen feet had become a required decompression stop. Without pre-dive planning, I had no idea how long we would have to stay. We made three stops at ten-foot intervals beginning at thirty feet. At the ten-foot level, we hovered until our air pressure was down to five hundred pounds. John seemed eager to surface, but I held on to him and gave him a stern look. If we were to get hit with the bends, it would happen right when we got to the surface or shortly thereafter. John wrenched himself out of my reach and surfaced while I stayed and sucked another hundred pounds of air.

Deep diving entices divers to danger, and the awaiting narcosis saturates the mind, deadening the vital attention to safety. No one escapes the effects of narcosis, that rapture of the deep where the sense of euphoria strips a mind of its sense of time and ability to make good judgments.

Back on the boat, I pulled John aside. "You know, when you decided to go deeper, we were already at the bottom time limit. Your move put us into decompression mode."

"No problem. I knew what I was doing. We were fine. Don't sweat it."

"John, what you did was reckless. We're both divemasters and we know better. Your decision to go deeper dragged me into the same risk zone as you."

"You could have headed back up without me. I'm not responsible for you, so don't put that on me," John said. He smiled and slapped me on the shoulder and returned to the others.

I stood, stunned by his dismissive attitude. I never dove with him again.

One never knows where the bends will hit the body or how severe the damage will be. A "hit" could come to a finger joint where it will eventually go away, or it can go into the soft tissue of the spinal cord and leave a diver paralyzed for life. Decompression sickness, the bends, "getting a hit"… call it what you will. This stuff is serious.

I sat out the rest of the dive trip. John resumed diving, scoffing at the risk of getting the bends and demonstrating bad diving habits to his other buddies. His goal was to become a divemaster at a Caribbean dive resort. With his sloppy and irresponsible habits, I doubt if he could have held a position at any reputable resort. Like me, none of the other divemasters on our weekend trip dove with him again.

Although I blamed John for abandoning the "buddy system," it was me who had allowed him to go in the first place. I knew narcosis had numbed my senses, yet I didn't heed its warning and allowed John to do the "thinking" for both of us. The more I thought about the incident, the more I blamed myself. Like it or not, we have great responsibility for our dive buddy's actions.

I used my experience for a roundtable discussion in one of my classes. "Here's the story and the situation. Should you stick with your buddy and place yourself in danger, go to the surface and allow your buddy to fend for himself, or do something else?" My students' perspectives varied widely, but they concluded that being a dive buddy is as much a moral and ethical matter as it is safe practice.

ROMANTIC OCTOPUSES

DIVE LOG

Date: August 1988
Location: Isla San Pedro Nolasco, Sea of Cortez, Mexico

Can an octopus feel? Can it feel love? If not, what did I just witness?

All quiet in the still water but for the omnipresent crackling of shrimp picking morsels out of the passing sea. This area is replete with octopuses that could be found with a minimally trained eye. I soon encountered two of them sitting next to each other. It was always a sign of a sharp eye to see an octopus and show it to other divers before it returned to its home. Being so out in the open would make this an easy trophy to claim.

As I approached, the octopuses fled to separate niches in the granite but remained vulnerable. I tried to work one out of its protective crevice, but it kept blasting me with a strong squirt of water from its siphon. It was stubborn. If I were to capture it, I would have to sit back and wait it out. So that's what I did.

I know you're uttering or thinking bad things about me, like, "You terrible beast. Why couldn't you just leave it alone?" Please, stay with me.

A tentacle protruded, sensing for danger as it stretched four or five inches. Soon a tentacle stretched out of the hiding place of the second octopus. Both tentacles explored the ocean floor, searching for each other. The arms stretched farther and farther, becoming as thin as pencil lead. They touched. Their arms intertwined and caressed each other as if to say, "I'm OK."

I came to this ocean as a visitor and found myself being taught one of the most important lessons about trespassing in a home not mine, and it was found in the gentle touching of the two octopuses.

I backed off. I was ashamed of my intrusiveness and hostile behavior.

The octopuses tentatively emerged from their shelters. They joined each other and rubbed their arms all over each other as if glad to be together again and safe. They studied me for a few minutes and left.

My encounter was a privilege. It was the first and only time I had observed any glimpse of feelings displayed between two sea creatures not engaged in sexual foreplay. I never molested an octopus again. I learned that if I wanted to touch one, I should move my hand slowly and close, then leave the next step of touching to the octopus.

Diving and underwater behavior have both come a long way since I began diving in 1980. I was taught to dive during a "come and pillage" era. We sat on barrel sponges for pictures. We turned rocks over to find small creatures, and then cut them up just to watch fish swoop in for a free meal. We took from the ocean whatever we wanted because we could. Of all that I wrote in this edition, this paragraph is the most embarrassing of all stories. We didn't know better even though common sense tells us that our actions were destructive.

It took two small octopuses to change my perspective on Planet Ocean and begin respecting that it is ours only to visit, but never to take from. Great lessons in life come from the least likely places. For me, it came from two octopuses.

HIS BRIDE LOST AT SEA

DIVE LOG

Date: June 1990
Location: Jado Trader, Guanaja, Honduras

Rough seas and a rolling up-current made everyone queasy. I waited in the corner of the boat, hoping I could get in before mal-de-mer got me. Had I not been sick, someone would have died.

This was my third trip to this resort on the Bay Islands, a chain of half a dozen volcanic islands piercing the northern coast of Honduras. How I found this place is another story, but what I found here was a paradise of its own.

The two-day trip to Guanaja (wha-nah-ha) was exhausting. The route from Phoenix required an overnight stay in Houston. The next morning began a series of plane changes and landing at airports that became nothing more than grass strips. The closer I got to my destination, the smaller the planes, the less English, and the more chickens aboard. DC-3 airplanes were the avionic workhorses of choice. The Central and South American governments bought thousands of them when they were decommissioned after World War II and the Korean Conflict. They were hardworking planes whose engines made a distinct sound to validate their power and reliability. They had round noses and small tail wheels. When boarding, you had to bend over and climb up the aisle, which was at a ten-degree angle. One plane I boarded had a pull rope to help hoist passengers to the front seats. They were slow, but they always got me there. Eventually most of them vanished. The airstrip on Guanaja was too short for the DC-3. We had to transfer to something made in Brazil.

Guanaja is typical of Honduran terrain. It is actually two islands separated by a man-made channel wide enough for two small boats to pass. The grass landing strip was right next to the channel.

Getting to Guanaja at the same time as gear was always part of the adventure. The simple yet reliable baggage system always haunted the type-A traveler. Tags on checked equipment were color-coded to the final destinations. La Ceiba—red. San Pedro Sula—blue. Guanaja—green. They counted the number of colored tags several times during the journey—at the check-in counter, when they were loaded on the plane, and then at each interim destination. If all the counts matched, the plane was given the go to fly to the next destination and almost everyone was happy. Mostly the system worked, but every now and then one of the airline agents became distracted and a yellow tagged bag flew off with the green group. Eventually luggage and passenger were reunited. I had greater faith in that system than the automated one in our country. When traveling to the dive destination, there was always that tense moment when my gear was the last bag off the plane.

The aerial view on approach was spectacular. Calm blue water on the lee. Turquoise near the shoreline that outlined the fringe reef. Suddenly we found ourselves between the two mountains on our final approach. The wind direction and velocity shifted dramatically, and the mountains of Guanaja created a wind tunnel effect. The plane, smooth flying one minute, abruptly shifted and bounced and dropped and swayed coming through the cut. It could quickly overtake an unsuspecting pilot. Landing was always a white-knuckle experience for the first-time visitor.

This travel day was almost over. The sun faded slowly in a blood-red western sky. A strong cool wind blew from the east. The arrival of the plane was a community social event. It brought loved ones, tourists, work, food, provisions, and mail. Locals flooded the landing strip to meet people and unload gear to a cart that resembled something from a 1940s American train station. The luggage cart was piled high and carefully rolled down a hill by a dozen local boys to ensure it didn't get away from them and end up in the water.

The helpers, mostly young boys aged ten to twenty, all had their hands on the cart to attest to their individual effort, thus earning a dollar for their work. All chattered at once in rapid Spanish that was most characteristic of Hondurans. Understanding any of them was difficult, but I suspect the oldest appointed himself supervisor and dictated terms to the others on how he would distribute tips. On the "dock"—planks held up by tree limbs in the shallows—helpers removed luggage and distributed it to various boats.

There was a group heading to the same resort as me. Very lively bunch. All were there for a wedding.

The resort was another one of my homes. I greeted and hugged the locals as I gave them gifts of pens, hard candies, shoes, and a Honduran country flag to replace the wind-whipped one on the dock flagpole. It was good to see the young ones—how they had grown. We were all told to find our rooms, relax, and meet at the bar for drinks and orientation.

This place was magical. It was warm and filled with a tropical sensation. The perpetual sound of the wind swept across the giant leaves of the banana trees. Falling mangos landed 'round the clock with distinctive *clunks* on the deck near the bar. There were birds—parrots, blackbirds with strange-looking tails, and the brilliantly colorful red and blue quetzal with long flowing tail.

I met the wedding party. Will and his bride-to-be, Sue. When they learned this was my third visit, they surrounded me and asked questions about the place and the diving. My previous trips made me a member of their group.

All right, enough background. Since this is a story about Sue, allow me to make the introduction.

* * *

Sue was a tall, blond, true-blue Texas shit-kicking beer-drinking hee-hawing two-steppin' country woman. She was self-assured and moved about with the sense of being comfortable with who she was. That's all anyone needs to know about her.

Sunday was the first day of diving. The stiff easterly breeze kicked up a choppy whitecap sea. It was not good water for a first dive to shake off the "winter jitters." The boat motored through the narrow channel to the lee side of the island where land protected us from wind and high seas. It was characterized by a shallow reef and volcanic catacombs teeming with fish and ribbons of light through holes in the ceiling. At the end of the dive day, I headed for the shady part of the boat. Sue and Will stood on the dive platform, sipping beer while chatting with friends in their wedding party.

Monday. The wedding day. Wind still blowing strong. Seas high. First-day dive jitters were declared "over." It was time for the real stuff. The windward side of Guanaja was a place for advanced divers.

The boat headed for the protective cays surrounding southern Guanaja. Our boat headed through a cut and out into the open Atlantic. Head winds and high seas challenged the most solid of stomachs. Projectile vomit spewed everywhere. I kept an eye on the horizon to stave off mal-de-mer creeping up on me.

The boat stopped. The divemaster grabbed a mooring line, and the skipper shut down the engine. It was quiet all around except for breaking whitecaps and moaning people. We donned equipment and listened to the dive briefing. Someone said, "Hurry. It's getting hot in these wet suits, and someone is going to get really sick in all this rocking and rolling."

I was ready to get in, but a dozen divers ahead blocked the doorway to the sea. Had to wait my turn. I was usually fast at getting ready and near the first to jump in. It was too dangerous that day to roll off the side. I simply had to wait.

The boat rocked, and my stomach began to surrender to seasickness, a rare event for me. I removed my equipment, took off my wet suit jacket, and sat down with eyes closed. Maybe I could ride it out. The clammy feeling began to subside, and it was a good time for a quick doze.

"Heffe, Heffe. No vas a bucear?" The skipper rousted me from my semi-stupor. The boat was empty except for the two of us. Did I not want to dive? he inquired. I leapt to my feet, donned my dive gear, and moved to the dive platform. *Get ready,* Jado Trader, *here I come!*

The *Jado Trader* was a sunken ship sitting in 110 feet of water. I had been there a few years ago when it first became a dive site. It was interesting to monitor the coral growth. Finding the group would be easy; just follow the mooring line down.

I was on the platform, ready to plunge in, when two divers surfaced about a hundred feet behind the boat. *What are they doing way back there?* They were too far out in deep water. It would be impossible for them to swim back to the boat against the wind, current, and waves, which had grown to four feet. Still, they attempted the surface swim. "Donde esta la línea de seguridad?" [Where is the security line?] I barked to the skipper. He scrambled to find the safety tag line. The divers separated. *Now what the hell are they doing?*

It was Will and Sue. I watched as Will left Sue and swam against the strong sea to the boat. Sue floated, flailing in the angry water. Both were now in serious trouble. Will got within range of the tag line, and the skipper threw it near him. We pulled him in. He was coughing and gasping for air.

"What is going on?" I yelled as I watched Sue continue to flail.

"Current too strong. Can't swim against it. Came back for line. Can't go out there. Too exhausted." He turned and looked back at his bride, and he choked and coughed. "I can't get to her." Will put his head on his arms in a sense of personal failure and despair.

I unbuckled my BC and tank, and it crashed to the deck. My weight belt fell nearby. Grabbing the tag line, I jumped into the water with mask and fins, and swam toward Sue. Time had been lost getting Will back to the boat and assessing the situation. Sue was growing smaller and smaller as she drifted farther away. But she was still flailing. That was the only good sign. As long as she flailed, she was alive.

Don't call me no hero. I was a dive instructor and fully trained in rescue techniques, and there was no one left on the boat to help Sue.

The rolling sea put me in troughs and crests. When your eyes are only an inch above the water, a four-foot swell looks like a giant wall of water. It was impossible to keep an eye on Sue's whereabouts. I turned to the skipper and raised questioning arms. He pointed. I followed his lead. Since I could not see over the swells, I stuck my head under water, hoping to spot her. She was fifteen feet away. Legs down. Not good. It meant she could sink. Her head was still above water, but time was running out. If she sank, I might not be able to free-dive down to her.

I reached the end of the safety line and let go. The seas and wind kept pushing Sue farther and farther away. Suddenly she vanished. I waited for the seas to put me on a crest. Had she gone down? Again I searched under water and found her only a few feet away. She was still floating, but motionless. Water flowed over her head. Her regulator was out of her mouth. I was too late—just moments too late. She was gone. What would I tell her groom?

What I'm about to tell you took an instant to happen. The mind works infinitely faster than we can act.

The world moved into slow motion and went silent. Even the sea seemed soundless. I could not hear the wind. Everything just stopped. The churning sea was no longer a threat to Sue.

I felt alone. Incredibly alone. Alone with a lifeless body whose spirit was gone. As peace came over Sue, so it overcame me. Could not see the boat. Didn't bother to look around for it. Who cares? I had failed. My sense of urgency ended. Had I abandoned Sue by spending too much time on the boat instead of acting? What were her last thoughts? Would they find me? What would they think? I had failed Will. I could not save his bride.

Something buoyed me up. It was the physics of the tumultuous sea. What prevented Will and Sue from descending became the energy that would hold us on the surface. Time returned me to the moment. I grabbed Sue and pulled her close. She was still breathing! Was life still there or was my denial of her death deceiving me?

I looked for Sue's regulator and found it in her stretched-out hand. I stuffed it in her mouth just as another wave broke over her head.

"Sue! Sue! Stay with me!"

She breathed!

I hunted for the purge valve to pump air into her BC and found it in her other hand—stretched out. I filled her BC with air and dropped her weight belt. Her legs floated to the surface. Sue was buoyant and safe.

"Sue, you're going to be OK! I've got you! Nod if you can hear me."

There was no response except for the wonderful sound of a working regulator pushing air into her lungs.

She was in my care now. I had been sent that day to be her keeper. In all my diving, this was the only time I was the last one off the boat. Had I not been feeling the mal-de-mer, this might have been a different story.

I looked for the boat. Every now and then I could see a speck of it toward the east. Could see no one on board. Divers were still down. It would be a while before it arrived.

I looked westward to see where we were being blown. We were being pushed toward Kaitron's Cay. I looked back for the boat—still not moving, but now there were divers aboard. *What's taking them so long? Don't they have a diver recall system in place?*

Kaitron's Cay was surrounded by a protective shallow fringe reef. Time to think about plan B. The boat was still a long way off. We were being blown toward the reef. The situation was deteriorating. Not good, but I shouted assurances to Sue.

I've seen the tops of fringe reefs from below. Jagged. Cutting. Ruthless. If we got to the reef, perhaps we could surf over them and find ourselves in only a few feet of water. But Sue was still limp. Did I have the strength to hold us both safely?

I thought back to my near-disaster years before in Hawaii with the jagged volcanoes and cutting cliffs. *Keep your fins to the reef*, I remembered.

"Sue, there's a reef ahead. It's gonna get rough, but we can get through this. I've done it before. Are you OK?"

Still no response—just the sound of steady, heavy breathing through the regulator. She was hyperventilating. I could think of nothing to put it in check. It was sucking up her air. She had less than four hundred pounds, which should be enough on the surface for another ten to fifteen minutes. How fast would hyperventilating deplete it? "Sue, you must try to take slower breaths. Try, Sue. Try!" Would she have enough air? It didn't matter. It had to last. It was now the least of our new set of problems.

I looked back to the boat. Could see a bow wake. It was moving. Finally! *Soon they will be here.*

I felt the push of surge. New problem. It was surge created by the fringe reef, warning us that we were on the verge of becoming entangled in breaking waves. If the boat didn't come soon, we could be boiled in the breakers and torn apart on the jagged fringe reef. Fins-first were good fenders unless we got turned around. If that happened, we would be tossed around like potatoes in a garbage disposal.

The surge grew stronger and thrust us toward the reef with greater force. I looked down and could now see the bottom and the edge of the reef. If we could keep our fins between the reef and ourselves, we might come out of this unscathed, but then the reef would make a boat pickup impossible. Fins-first! Who would get to us first? *Hurry, boat!*

Growling engines were now within earshot. I raised my arm to pinpoint our location. The boat came straight at us. I wanted to keep my eye on the boat but had to prepare for the surf over the reef.

The boat turned. They threw a line. I grabbed it and held Sue tightly.

The pull on the line was forceful and comforting as the boat moved to deeper water.

The sea relentlessly cast its large swells and whitecaps. The stern of the boat plunged high and slapped deep into the water. As they pulled us closer, we still had to face the challenge of getting back on board.

"Espere la calma!" [Wait for the calm!] shouted Raul.

The platform became a giant flyswatter slapping at the rolling sea. "Espere!" yelled Raul again. Then the counterbalance of waves and the platform momentarily settled. Many hands pulled Sue to safety. Another large swell came. The platform sank below the raging water. I pushed Sue up, fully geared with scuba. They lifted her lifeless body out of the water.

It was now my turn to get on board.

My emotional battle was over, but my muscles were spent. I could not pull myself up, and all the divers had turned their attention to Sue. Suddenly there was a large swell, the stern plunged deep below the surface, and it was as though hands lifted me into the boat. Could it have been my Maker?

They stripped Sue of her gear, covered her in towels, and administered oxygen. Her wedding party stood around wanting to help but not knowing what to do. Sue was safe. We headed for home.

I huddled unnoticed at the stern of the boat, trying to catch my breath. Knees up, arms draped over them to hold an exhausted head.

The boat sided to the pier. The entire wedding party got off. They had a wedding to attend later that day, and the bride had come close to missing it.

Me? I recuperated quickly and was ready for my first dive of the day. That nasty mishap was over—let's get back to why we're here. The boat left with only Raul and me to Beginner's Reef, another challenging spot on that wind-blown sea. There was diving to do. Let's go.

***

Later that afternoon I heard knocking at my door. Sue gave me a hug and thanked me. Until she recovered, she did not learn who her rescuer was. She invited me to the festivities. I never pass up the chance for a good shindig. None of her group knew I was invited, and one guest gave me a scornful look for crashing their party.

I learned that when Will and Sue went back to Texas, they took a self-rescue course, but never dove again.

I kept in touch with Sue. Her business occasionally took her to California, and she would arrange a layover in Phoenix to give us time to sit in the airport bar and clank beer mugs.

Then one day there came a letter from Will. Sue was gone—taken by the cancer beast. I was overcome by the news and sat weeping in the corner of my backyard. That day at sea had formed bonds, and when Sue left, part of me went with her.

I played that day over and over and decided it had to be a miracle that I was the only diver left on the boat and the only one with rescue experience. An accident or a stroke of luck, some might say. Strange how all these accidents in life may not be accidents at all. Maybe it is all part of a great plan none of us understand without the aid of our spiritual beliefs. I wonder about the intricacies of those "accidental" brief encounters that create memories that last forever and end up in stories like these long after the day is done.

Seasickness is a never-ending scourge for divers. Only once did it ever hit me so hard that I almost sat out a dive. That would have been dive 310, the one that never happened on June 7, 1990. It was that non-dive that became among the most memorable of all.

THREE FAT CHICKS

TRAVEL JOURNAL

Date: September 1993
Location: Sand Castles, San Salvador, Bahamas

They were not giddy; they just found everything funny. When I asked if I could join them, I immediately wondered how I was going to politely excuse myself from the three fat chicks who laughed loudly at stories involving dead or dying people.

Clint was tall and handsome. His six-foot, three-inch structure spent workdays flinging timber and beams and bundles of plywood on the roofs of new homes. He was a framer. He did the heavy work. He hammered and carried timbers around from daybreak to sunset—five days a week all year long. At the end of the day he stopped at a pub and slammed beer glasses with his buddies until closing time. Clint was all iron. A simple handshake could crush all twenty-seven bones in my hand. He had a good job. It paid him well. Had his health. Had looks. Had his freedom. He was a true man's man. But this is not a story about Clint.

Three women huddled around the pay phone in the Fort Lauderdale Executive Jet Center. One spoke while the other two pressed their ears toward the receiver to hear the other end of the conversation. Their spokesperson talked with a calming voice. I thought it a curious scene. But it was not my place to eavesdrop.

I heard my name come over the PA system. It was time to board the nine-passenger charter airplane for the three-hour jaunt over the waters of the Bahama Banks to the Riding Rock Inn on San Salvador—360 miles in a southwesterly direction.

Once we landed, there was talk about some guests arriving without their luggage. Their gear hadn't made the mainland connection. *Poor bastards*, I thought. I'd had it happen to me a few times. Not a good feeling. Very empathetic for the victims. I wondered who they were.

After settling in, most guests wandered over to the Riding Rock Inn's well-known Driftwood Bar. Noise levels increased as more people arrived. Soon the place was packed elbow to elbow with divers giving their weeklong holiday a kick-start.

The door burst open. In walked three giggling, jovial women. They were the same women I had seen earlier that day crowding around the pay phone in Florida. It was plain their party had started much earlier. Didn't take them long to make themselves at home in the crowd. Rum punch flowed, and everyone became instant pals.

Clint approached, motioned with his head to where the three ladies were standing, and with a quiet voice made comments about those "three fat chicks." I looked at Clint, looked toward the women, and said nothing.

Saturday afternoon dive orientation came with endless rum punches, conch fritters, the rules for having fun, and boat assignments. Clint approached me again, chuckling. "I'm sure glad those three fat chicks weren't assigned to our boat. All that body mass would sink us for sure."

I glanced over to the ladies. Clint's remarks were unwelcome. My silence was not enough to give him the hint. This needed something more direct. A large rock, perhaps.

I reached for another rum punch and slalomed my way through the packed room to the three ladies huddled at the end of the bar. They were friendly and obviously glad to have their weeklong holiday off to a good start. I introduced myself. Meet Sadie, Phyllis, and Doris. They were, indeed, large women, and their smiles and warm eyes were equally large. They were definitely here to have fun.

"I heard some of the guests' gear did not arrive from Fort Lauderdale," I said to keep a conversation going. They laughed at once as if someone had pushed the giggle button.

"We did, too. It was ours."

"So that's what you were on the phone about back in Fort Lauderdale. Did you get any indication of when it would get here?"

They shrugged. One of them said, "It'll get here, or it won't. We have plenty of deodorant, our bathing suits, and can survive the week in what we're wearing. The manager told us they would give us rental gear until ours came. So we're set!" They clinked their glasses and sent out a resounding "Yahoo!"

Sunday morning brought the first day of a new dive week. Amidst the confusion and first-day dive jitters, everyone managed to get themselves and their gear on the right boat. I was on the boat with about eight or nine others, and the three ladies had a second boat all to themselves. They laughed and waved as they called to us to have fun on our dive. Their boat left the marina.

Clint stood up, watching the boat leave. "Of course their boat got off to an early start; there were only three fat chicks aboard. It's unsafe to put too much weight on deck. That boat's gonna capsize." Some people aboard our boat laughed, some smiled, but mostly no one said anything as they turned their eyes away.

Who were these ladies? No one else knew their names. Clint's persistence prevented others from seeing the humans living in those bodies. Clint effectively stripped Sadie, Phyllis, and Doris of their right to be viewed as sensitive, feeling people. They became three fat chicks, and in others' eyes, soon ceased being people at all. Fat people, Clint reasoned, couldn't possibly feel fear, pain, or joy. We denude the value in others with persistent name-calling—especially of those who are different from us. It's an age-old hate tactic.

* * *

At the end of the dive day, I wandered up the path to the inn. The three ladies stood in the pool, continuing with their quiet stories and breaking out in loud laughter. How could they have such good attitudes when their gear was somewhere else? If only I could learn their secret.

"May I join you?" I looked on from the edge of the pool. They opened their circle and welcomed me in. After reintroductions, they resumed their stories and simultaneously broke into loud laughter. They told tales about the dead or dying. How could I politely excuse myself? They were just as bad as Clint. How could I have been offended with Clint only to be drawn to these women who were even more offensive?

Suddenly they stopped jiving and looked at me. There seemed to be a mental telepathy of signals among them. Phyllis spoke. "There's something you should know about us. We're nurses. We work the second shift emergency room in the Boston City Hospital. We get the worst of the worst. We get the dead, the dying, the drunks, the ones with gaping holes from gunshot wounds and the ones bleeding to death from knife slashes. We get those who OD on drugs. We get the battered women. We get the DUIs who survive car wrecks. We get the ones who lose in the gang fights. In a week we see more violent death than seasoned soldiers see in an entire war. We see it day after day, week after week. It would be easy to become lost in the ugly side of life. It would be easy to go insane with it all. We release by telling these morbid stories. We find young nurses crouched in broom closets puking their guts out, crying in despair about the lost world and without the strength to even continue their shift. Weekends are the worst. If we did not joke about the dead or dying to release what we see, we'd become the insane beasts you see in the streets, and then there would be no one to help them."

Holy crap!!

"Why do you do it, then?"

"Because we save lives. We bring nearly dead people back to life to give their miserable souls one more chance to do it right. Some get it together. Most don't. We do what God wants us to do. Ours is not a job. It's a calling. It's what we were born to do. And we are not the least bit sorry for having chosen the careers we have."

Holy more crap!!

"So… you're nurses. Maybe you can help me. My daughter is attending a two-year nursing program and is thinking about attending a four-year program. What's your advice on this?"

They sang in unison, "Tell her to get into the four-year course." When I asked why, they spent the next half hour giving me a long list of reasons.

I fell in love with them all. They laughed easily. They didn't take themselves seriously. They didn't get worked up over stuff that doesn't seem to matter. They were practical. They may have sounded hard, but inside they were empathetically gushy.

* * *

Divers sauntered down to the marina after their lunch nap. Clint pointed to the other boat. "Look there, see how the boat lists to one side? That's why that boat has so few people on it. Those fat chicks are a safety hazard."

I snapped. "That's enough! Do you know who they are? What they do? Do you know their names? Do you even care?"

"Hey! I was just having a little fun. Lighten up!"

"Lighten up? Look what you're doing. You've poisoned many of the others on this boat by calling them 'three fat chicks.' Maybe you should find out who they are. You're just having a little fun, eh? Well, you know where you can shove it. Hell, I need to get off this boat."

The divemaster yelled to the captain of the other boat. The ladies seemed delighted to have new company as they watched me bring my gear aboard.

The boat ride to the dive site was short. We dropped anchor and the divemaster gave a quick briefing. The second dive boat headed directly toward us and slowed down as if it were going to bring something or deliver a message.

"What's going on with them?" Doris said.

"Maybe they're coming to tell us our gear got here," Sadie said.

When the other boat was about thirty feet off our stern, all the male divers stood on the benches, turned, dropped their trunks, and mooned the ladies as they passed.

There was a momentary silence.

Then the women shouted and gave wolf whistles. They yelled and beckoned to them to return and do it again.

We watched. And waited.

The boat turned. The ladies cheered. The guys lined up on the benches—preparing for another mooning. Just before the boat passed, the women rolled straps off their shoulders and snatched their swimsuits down to their waists. They stood tall, yelling and yahooing. I had never seen so many pounds of breast swaying in the afternoon sun as I did that day at Sand Castles.

Shockwaves silenced everyone on the other boat. There was no encore mooning. They steered straight as the women continued to cheer and wave their arms wildly over their heads. They laughed so hard, they started coughing.

"I guess that shut 'em up," Phyllis said.

Sadie and Doris pulled their swimsuits back up, and the three continued dive preparations. "Ahem! Ahem! Phyllis. Oh, Phyllis," Sadie and Doris sang. Phyllis looked up at Sadie. "Phyllis, do you plan to put your swimsuit back on or are you going to just stand there embarrassing Jeff?"

Phyllis looked down at herself and then looked at me and chuckled. "This bother you?"

"Hey, if guys can go without a shirt, girls can, too."

"Ladies, I think I'll just dive topless," Phyllis announced. They broke out into another laugh.

"Well, if you're gonna do it, so are we," said Doris.

The ladies stepped off the back dive platform. I looked to the boat captain, shrugged, and rolled my eyes. "Could you please hand me my camera when I get in?"

The water was clear and warm. Always a favorite dive spot. Always looked so inviting. I snapped macro pictures of small critters on the mounds of coral.

The women swam my way, wanting to capture the Kodak moment. They crowded together, proudly exposing their chests. Copious breasts floated without the pressure of gravity and took on a natural and beautiful form. I had to grin. They were full of endless surprises. With all this and their captivating personalities, they were sure a handsome lot. I motioned for them to huddle closer as I pointed the camera their way. The shutter snapped and the strobe flashed. They waved and swam off.

Back on the boat, the ladies were no longer concerned about modesty and extended the stay of their newfound freedom.

"When we get back, I'll give you an address so you can send a copy of the picture," Phyllis said.

"You're going to be disappointed. I rigged the camera for macro photography, and anything beyond three inches won't be anything more than a blur."

There was silence, and then they burst into their usual spontaneous laughter.

"I wonder what they're saying on the other boat," Doris said. "You can bet they have some things to say about what we did."

"Couldn't be any worse than what they've been saying all week," Phyllis added.

"Wait," I said. "You know what they were saying?"

"When someone's watching you and motioning with his head while speaking softly to others, you know he's making fun," Phyllis replied. "Who is that tall guy anyway?"

The bosom-flashing incident became the table-talk that night. Most of the guests were more animated and jovial. Loud talking saturated the dining room. More people began greeting my three friends, and soon everyone was laughing at the same silly things the ladies did.

Their gear eventually arrived, but almost too late to bother unpacking.

I never got an address for Phyllis. The picture did turn out as an indiscernible blur. It would have been fun to send it anyway. I would have heard them laughing all the way to Phoenix.

Clint never made another comment, and my three friends stopped being the three fat chicks. He went back to his eastern town and to his hammer and beer-drinking buddies. I heard he fell smitten with a fair maiden and married, and to this day he treats her like a queen and pampers her with an enviable tenderness.

***

My daughter decided to become a registered nurse, went on to a four-year nursing college, and worked in the intensive care unit. She told me stories about how they cluster in the break rooms late at night telling morbid jokes about the dead to keep their sanity, and how they become a sisterhood for other nurses who "lose it."

From time to time my mind wanders back to the day I snapped at Clint. His venom didn't dampen the women's spirits. I have yet to understand how mocking others who are different from us makes us better. In Clint's effort to sway others, was he only trying to dilute or hide from his own insecurity? The week on San Salvador was a microcosm of human behavior. It had demonstrated the power of negative influence and how quickly the family of man can heal when the stick of hatred is taken from those who hate themselves the most.

THE LAST BOAT RIDE

TRAVEL JOURNAL

Date: July 1994
Location: Tilloo sandbar, Bahamas

We headed out of the harbor at first light. Dottie was at my side. The turquoise backdrop of Tilloo lay hidden in dawn, and I thought I would never see its splendor again.

She had been gone for years, and the plastic urn had sat ominously on the shelf long enough. Deciding to take Dottie to Tilloo was an act of closure. Most governments get fidgety about bringing a person's remains into or out of their countries. Bringing Dottie's ashes into the Bahamas required dozens of forms, official stamps, hit-or-miss communication with officials, hefty fees, and rules about the box I would carry her in. Unwilling to tolerate the bureaucracy, I smuggled her in—deep in my gear and undetectable.

Once through immigration, I picked up my boat and motored to Tilloo in the early light of dawn. I came without a plan for a ceremony, knowing that something fitting and unforgettable would come to mind. I sat quietly in the boat, pondering the path that had brought me to that moment.

It was alcoholism that took her. Through her disease, Dottie gave up on herself, but in my ignorance and frustration I gave up on us. I made ours a fifty-fifty relationship, demanding that she meet me halfway at a time when she needed help the most. Fifty-fifty relationships aren't good enough. What happens if the other person can't show up?

How can you be sure you can show up yourself? I feared that my sin of abandonment would return to haunt me for the rest of my days. Whatever good that might come along on my path… I figured I didn't deserve It. We learn the best from loss, and this is the second-greatest travesty of life. The first is learning nothing at all.

I slipped into the warm waters and stood waist-deep, sobbing as her ashes fell through my fingers, creating a half-moon smile in the sand below. Within moments Planet Ocean covered them, and they were protected by the perpetually cleansing hands of the sea. Goodbye, my love. Goodbye. Goodbye. Goodbye.

REMEMBER A MOONBEAM

Moonbeams…
They awaken and drench you.
Their soft light tickles and plays with you.
Sensuous caresses torment you,
Tempting you, teasing you.
The moon wants to see, and touch.
Stand in its glow.
Be seduced.

Awaken, my love!
Feel my lingering fingers.
You reach, wanting more.
Carried away with ecstasy.
But now you are gone from the world,
Leaving me here… alone with my moonbeams.

Stand by the window and kiss me goodnight.
Press my hand to your breast once more before you go.
My moonbeams.
They remain and linger like my touches.
Reminding me of you long after you are gone.

SABOTAGED!

TRAVEL JOURNAL

Date: September 1995
Location: Split Reef, San Salvador, Bahamas

Had I been of sound mind, Pam would have become my permanent partner. She was in constant search of a new opportunity to surprise me. She was quick to enter the water and wait for me at the bottom. When I caught up with her, I found her waiting with three newfound friends who had dropped in unexpectedly.

Pam was already a certified diver, but she needed retraining after a decades-long hiatus. Before heading to the islands, I took her through a pool refresher to reunite her with the wonder of diving, reacquaint her with the skills, and give me the confidence that she would be a comfortable and competent companion in the ocean. Her skills returned quickly. She had good form, followed safe diving practices, and watched her gauges.

As instructor, I taught my students that good boat etiquette commands that divers not approach the dive platform unless they are ready to go down. Loitering on the surface is taboo. Get out or get down. Pam never lingered on the dive platform or floated around on the surface.

***

Split Reef was a poor excuse for a dive spot. To exceed depths of twenty feet at Split Reef, one had to bring a shovel. In the "old days" of the 1980s, before dive computers, the US Navy Air Dive Tables governed our dive depths, bottom times, and surface intervals. This dive site was so shallow it was almost impossible to get decompression sickness. Since there wasn't much here except dead or dying coral and a conspicuous absence of fish life, sites like this became known as "blow off dives." A part of the reef had been used as a conch shell dump site, and that was the extent of its attractions. To the west of the reef was the abyss with its blue glow luring divers to explore the wall, but that was forbidden on this shallow dive.

* * *

The pre-dive briefing was brief. "Here we are, folks, at Split Reef. This is a shallow dive. You can see we anchored between two small reefs, one to the left"—pointing—"and the other to the right"—more pointing—"and that's how this place got its name. There is sand down there. You can see it right below the boat. There is no current. Water temperature here is probably 85 degrees. Go where you want but stay off the wall. Last week we saw hammerheads here. Pool's open. Have a good dive."

Last week we saw hammerheads here??!! In dive briefing vernacular, that means "this is a crappy dive site." Too often, I have heard divemasters say, "There were sharks and turtles at this very spot last week." Their hope was to excite divers into thinking we might get to see one of these magnificent creatures. I have never seen turtles or sharks on any of the dives where they told us to keep a sharp eye out for them.

Except for the hammerhead shark comment, the briefing confirmed what I had told Pam about this being an uneventful dive. "If this site is really as bad as you say, let's make it a photo dive," she said. "I'd like to send something back to Mom and Dad."

"OK, when you go in, I'll just follow you and snap the entire roll. Just swim around and ignore me. You'll look more natural."

Pam decided to dive without a wet suit. She donned her gear and said she would go in first and get ready for the photo shoot. She jumped into the water, signaled she was descending, and disappeared. I hustled to catch up. I rolled over the side and headed down. The boat swung on its anchor, scattering divers like feed in the chicken yard. I spotted Pam almost fifty feet away. All the divers went in front of the boat. Pam was far to the back and close to the forbidden wall.

She waited patiently, gazing out over the wall until I caught up with her. She turned toward me and proudly bared her breasts while she waved her bikini top around in the water like a ribbon. She wore a grin to commemorate the surprise and seemed quite pleased with my reaction to her tight-fitting and shapely birthday suit. I should not have been surprised, because Pam always looked for a way to catch me off guard.

* * *

Pam was more than a dive buddy. She was my significant other for several years. She was my friend in the best of ways. She helped me through my demon era and was my support group.

She was a beautiful woman. Her parents were of German ancestry. Her two younger sisters looked German. Pam looked Middle Eastern. She had high cheekbones and olive skin that browned up under the Arizona sun. Her emerald-green eyes sparkled and flirted with life itself.

She made it a priority to tease me with looks, risqué clothing, and stolen touches in public places.

Pam despised the constriction of clothing—preferred to wear little or nothing at all. Within five minutes of being home, she traded work clothing for a blouse left blatantly unbuttoned. In public she was careful. She explained that although she would seek the freedom of nudity, she was not an exhibitionist. She rebelled against rules made for the sake of rules. She always took the dare and dared me to take a step away from my culture of cautious conventionalism. She challenged others to think differently. Pam was her own person. And she gave herself to me. Completely.

* * *

Pam hovered over the edge of Split Reef. Ribbons of sunbeams tantalized her skin like soft laser lights in a smoke-filled New Orleans jazz club. The azure blue glow of the abyss became the studio backdrop. And here I thought we were going to take pictures for Mom and Dad.

Suddenly becoming a mermaid was a little out of character since we were among other divers, which, by her definition, made this a public place. I discovered over time that her definition of *public* was fluid and based on both appropriateness and proximity. Not to worry about *public* here. Divers tend to be preoccupied with diving and are surprisingly unobservant. Topless mermaids frequently go unnoticed. I often wondered why divers wear masks at all.

I readied the camera to frame the shot. Suddenly, three large hammerhead sharks emerged from the deep and swirled behind Pam. They were close enough to touch. The magnificence of the moment sidetracked my concentration. I lowered the camera to my side. Should have taken a picture. Pam looked around to see what I was watching with such intent and came eye to eye with the sharks as they turned to leave.

She looked up anxiously, the first sign of stress that comes moments before panic that triggers sudden moves, like bolting to the surface. Such reactions can result in air embolisms that are commonly fatal. I grabbed her fins to prevent a bad decision about to happen.

All Pam wanted to do was get out of the water. She continuously pointed to the surface. I held her tight and kept my face in hers until she settled down. Through our sign language, I convinced her that the fish were gone, and no harm would come to her unless she made an unwise attempt to surface. Pam put the distractions of sharks behind her and began enjoying the dive.

I have long told others about mermaids in the sea. One must be vigilant lest they be missed, and be gentle upon discovery so as not to frighten them away. Pam became a mermaid. She took to the freedom of water washing over her breasts and glided easily through the blue. In the sea, breasts take their natural shape. With her flawless dark olive skin, she was transformed into an alluring mermaid, leaving me a memory that was superior to any picture that could be captured on film.

Mermaids don't necessarily come with sensuous bodies and beautiful breasts. It begins in the soul where a person's attitude frees the spirit and their childlike nature can once again reign with the blessing of simplicity. Any damsel can expose her breasts under water. It is when she becomes emancipated to the boundlessness of freedom, liberated from the thoughts of others, and acts out her play that she becomes a true mermaid. Anything short of this is a sure sign of a counterfeit mermaid.

Time escaped. Time to return from the spell and head to the surface. Where was Pam's swimsuit top? We looked at each other as if simultaneously sensing where we could find it—on the bottom, where we'd met Pam's three friends. It was not snagged on the fringes of the reef. I looked into the deep. There it was, fifty feet below in the forbidden zone. In complying with safe dive practice, going for it was too risky.

We looked down to her top, then at each other, and then down again. Now what? We had to face the crowd on the boat. Pam, this person who preferred nudity to clothing but was no exhibitionist, pictured herself having to climb up the steps to the platform to look fifteen other people in the eye when they were not looking back at her green eyes. This was a situation that could bring anxiety to any girl. No one likes to be gawked at.

We drifted slowly to the surface. We approached the boat. I ran interference for my half-naked mermaid. Called to the divemaster and asked him to throw a T-shirt. Pam removed her gear, pulled the T-shirt over her head, and climbed back into her gear, and we headed for the boat.

Pam's modesty was safe. We climbed the ladder to the platform. They removed our gear. She turned to me with a smile and said, "Phew! That was close. I was wondering how we were going to pull that off."

"Um. Maybe you should take a look at yourself."

The T-shirt was wet and clung to her body. Being thin and white, it was transparent. It turned heads and silenced all talking. She spun on her heels, turning her back to them. "Oh, God! Now what?"

"Welcome to the world of diving," I said as I wrapped a towel around her. "Just laugh it off."

The crew pulled up the ladder, hoisted anchor, and headed in for lunch. We stood mesmerized, looking over the stern platform as the water glistened in the blue turquoise below. Split Reef would never be the same again. For us, it was an otherwise ordinary experience turned incredible.

As the week wore on, Pam pulled her top down to her waist on many dives. Her BC gave her marginal privacy from the side and none from the front. I convinced her no one would notice. During one dive she tested my observation. We swam toward others, waved to get their attention, and kept going. No diver ever noticed.

Pam and I had volumes of memories that would take us to the sunny side of the attic in our old age. My journals detail the stories of our passionate and spontaneous adventures while we laughed at the world for their fears at the voyages we sought.

Some wondered whatever became of us... such unimaginable romance. "It wasn't meant to be," I replied. Such a feeble dismissal that even I had difficulty believing. It took years before I could figure it out and some said I fell in love too soon. I lost Pam because I had convinced myself that I didn't deserve a compatible companion after I had lost my alcoholic spouse. With Pam, I sabotaged our relationship, our love, our future, our life. It became one of my most haunting regrets.

Demons come with life's package. They flourish on our foolish past and remind us of our trespasses. They punish and censure us for our imperfections. They leave only when we face what we strive to hide, forgive ourselves, and then send them away.

FLICKER IN THE NIGHT SKY

Have you ever lain on Mother Earth at night
Looking to the heavens—wondering about their depth?
Wondering where "there" is and how far away it could be?
Then, suddenly, there's a wisp of a flash before your eyes!

A shooting star!
A fleck of cosmic dust announcing its extinction.
One that lights up only an inch of the sky.
A space so small and so faint
That if your eyes were not looking at that exact spot,
The shooting star would never have been seen.

How many light-years upon light-years it traveled,
That tiny speck of sand?
Traveled to become a wink of light in the night sky
At that precise moment in time.
Have you ever wondered that, perhaps…
Perhaps it was sent just for you?
A speck of sand dashing across the galaxy
Made a million years ago.
Just for you.

So when I look upon you, my love,
I think of that shooting star.
One that raced through the heavens for light-years
And filled an inch of the night sky
Just to touch my eyes only.
The one made just for me
And that changed my life forever.

TITO, THE BOY FROM SAVANNAH BIGHT

TRAVEL JOURNAL

Date: May 1995
Location: Savannah Bight, Guanaja, Honduras

Luis picked us up to take us to his village, meet his family, and be his dinner guests. It was Labor Day in Guanaja (wha-nah-ha), and that gave the locals from Savannah Bight a reason to celebrate. I became immersed in their culture and was welcomed into their village, but my mastery of Spanish could never make me what I wanted to be.

The Posada del Sol, or the Posada, was a five-star dive resort on Guanaja, one of the islands in a group called the Bay Islands off Honduras. Luis was the boat captain of the Posada fleet. He could maneuver his boat with the precision of a surgeon. His was an honorable and prestigious profession. His skill earned him top pay, and his warm smile and desire to please always brought generous tips. In his village he was a young hero. He treasured his roots and respected the people who raised him. He generously shared what he had with anyone in need.

When I'd first met Luis, ten years earlier, he was a thin, lanky kid who had just begun working at the Posada as a groundskeeper. They gave him big black boots that were twice as large as his feet and came above his knees. Along the way he picked up the nickname Tito, Spanish for "uncle." He was a hard worker and approached every task with energy and a broad smile. In his bid to please, he was always enthusiastically willing to do whatever was asked.

And there he was, through the years, now a grown man. Black boots handed down to the children behind him, Luis progressed to the most coveted position a Honduran in that region could dare dream about—a boat captain for the Posada fleet.

It was a sign of manhood when a young Honduran could grow facial hair. Luis did all he could to muster that poor excuse for a beard. But in Central America, the quality of the beard was not the issue. Didn't matter. Hair was hair. And it made boys men.

To Luis, I was family and part of his forever past. Luis learned English well, but he saved it to practice on others so I could practice my Spanish on him. He was understanding and respectful in correcting my use of words and giving me ones that were a better fit for the local culture.

Savannah Bight was a small fishing village about five miles to the east of the Posada. Been many times near it but no time in it. A taxi boat shuttled dozens of people daily from Savannah Bight to Bonacca Town, a village built on sticks and a maze of boardwalks over the water. I worried about that taxi getting top heavy with people oozing over the sides and sitting on the canopy above the overstuffed cabin. It was an accident waiting to happen, but this was a developing country, and I heard the Lord doubles or triples the number of guardian angels assigned in these rural places.

Over time I learned about the Honduran culture. I learned how to act, to sit, to gesture, to talk, to eat. When Luis invited Peri and me to supper, not only did I feel honored for the invitation, but it was also a good test of my cultural and language skills.

Peri was a Stateside Posada employee who booked trips for guests. She was a pleasant and understanding telephone voice who had become my trusted friend and confidant. We checked in often through the years to trade stories of fallen loves and misplaced tragedies. While settling into my room on arrival day, I heard a welcoming voice. I had never met her in person, but that familiar voice could belong only to my friend Peri. What a surprise. *What brings her here?*

Peri was thin, with a lined face telling of her own life's adventures. She came from Turkish ancestry and had dark skin, black eyes, and a warming smile. She traveled to the Posada from time to time to inspect operations and validate the status reports sent Stateside. But, she revealed, the purpose of this trip was to come and see the face behind a voice on the telephone.

Although Peri and I had developed our own friendship, we both had close connections with Luis and were invited to his village to celebrate the Honduran Labor Day. We stood at the Posada dock waiting, and soon a boat approached. It was Luis.

Twenty minutes later we arrived at Savannah Bight. The village was larger than it looked from a distance. Luis lived in one of the many boxy homes perched on posts high over the water, each with an uneven, narrow dock. We tied the boat, climbed a makeshift ladder, and then a few steps farther and we were inside his home. It was the size of a two-car garage and divided into quarters without inside walls—part kitchen, part dining room, part living room, and part bedroom. Windows were openings with shutters hinged at the top to provide shelter, shade, and plenty of ventilation. The bathroom consisted of a privy, a bench with a sitting hole. Privacy was accomplished by a hanging blanket and politeness. Nothing sophisticated. Look down the hole to the sea. Flushed by the tide. Sanitation not an issue with the villagers.

In the middle of the house was a single light bulb with a pull string. Several plugs came from atop the bulb. One to a stereo and the other to the kitchen. Few had homes over the water *and* electricity. Most of the so-called developed world would call Luis' home a ghetto, but not here. He proudly invited guests into his.

Out the front door was a maze of planks that connected the stilt houses to one another and to dry land. Not a place for drunkenness. Easy to fall and be dashed by the rocky shore below. Carefree children jumped about, protected by that army of overworked guardian angels.

The village bulged with people sitting around on logs, hanging out windows, or propped up against huts. People watched people while talking with one another. Five hundred inhabitants called this village "home." Everyone knew one another, and most were somehow related. There was an endless supply of inebriated and curious Hondurans with bloodshot eyes and crooked teeth and dirty T-shirts filled with holes. And they all smelled bad. But generous were they with their smiles and hospitality. They surrounded us with their curiosity and enthusiasm for us to join their celebration.

Children exploded with excitement and ran to a man on a mule who had just arrived from the steep mountains surrounding the hidden village. Their hands reached to touch him and his mule. They all talked at once as the man moved slowly through the young mob. To them, he was a folk hero. Seemed like he had the only means of transportation that wasn't a boat. Bananas were his booty.

We walked with Luis while being introduced to sisters, brothers, cousins, aunts, and uncles. Luis and Peri left to get drinks, and I found myself encircled by villagers—all peppering me with questions about my homeland, my people, and how I had come to know Luis. They moved close to touch my clothing, my skin, my face, my hair. As foreign as they were to me, I was much more of an oddity to them.

I spotted the familiar face of a young man who was a deckhand at the Posada. He had light curly hair and fair skin, and I knew him to be a quiet one. He sat, lounging on an upside-down dory, sipping a beer while talking with another man. I knew he was not a Honduran but a Colombian who, as a toddler, had been adopted by the villagers when his family was killed in a boat accident. Something changed while watching him. He was all I could see. The villagers surrounding me seemed to disappear. Sound became faint noise. Seeing that young man was like watching a slow-motion movie. Life turned surreal. Like me, the young man was different from the villagers, yet he was one of them. I compared myself with him. I wore their clothing. I could speak their language. My tan made me as dark as them. I understood their customs. I walked in their towns and villages. But I would soon get on a boat and go back to my own world. Under the façade, my skin would always be white. I could never be one of them.

I had come to cultural maturity. It was both very humbling and devastating. These people had simple ways, pure hearts, and a genuine willingness to help their brothers. They learned to be happy with nothing, and in that, they found richness most of the Western world would never know. Foolishly, I thought that by my trying to become one of them, others would see that I belong to the brotherhood of honorable crusaders protecting the vanishing principles of honesty, respect, and consideration for others.

Cultural maturity dealt a devastating blow. I had spent years walking the wrong path.

Luis' family—it was beautiful. His young wife, Helena, didn't look a day over fifteen. She was small and frail looking, and wore a shy demeanor. There was no eye contact. She stayed close to Luis and said little.

Then there was Lisa, their four-year-old child, filled with endless energy and perpetual hope. It was easy to fall in love with her. She liked kicking Luis' prize soccer ball around the house. I asked Luis how he was able to keep it from flying out the back and vanishing into the sea. Moments later the ball whisked past my nose on a straight path toward the opening. There came a bloodcurdling shriek from Lisa. Luis calmly stuck his foot out, and the ball squirted back to Lisa. "You see," said Luis with his perpetual smile, "that's how it never gets lost."

Luis opened a beer, handed it to me, and invited Peri and me to watch the sunset on the dock while he cooked. I was almost afraid to drink the beer because it would trigger the need to pee through the hole in the privy and fall into the sea below and everyone would know what I was doing.

The sun sank behind the mountain across the bay. The clouds turned blood red. Then rust. Then the water mimicked the sky. Everything turned red as the day crashed in a theatrical ending. Peri and I sat speechless while being washed in the peace of these simple people, so happy with so little.

"Dinner's ready!" said Luis as he brought a plate teeming with fried fish. Fish was the main dish. And the appetizer. And the side dish. And dessert. It smelled scrumptious.

"What kind of fish is this, grouper?"

"No, it's barracuda."

Mentally, I panicked. *Barracuda? You can't eat barracuda! It will give you ciguatera poisoning! Its victims pray for death. There is no known cure. It is life debilitating. How could Luis do this to us? What do I do? How can I refuse his hospitality?* There was more food on that plate than most of the villagers saw in a week. Imagine the message it would send, coming all the way on a dinner invitation to see his village and then rejecting his food. Nonchalantly I asked, "How can you tell when barracuda is OK to eat?"

"Oh, that's easy," said Luis. "You just cut off a piece and feed it to your neighbor's dog. If it dies, the fish was bad, and you toss it." A twinkle appeared in his eye and a broad grin grew on his face. "You don't see too many dogs around here, do you?

"Actually," he continued, "we cut a piece and place it on a red ant hill. If the ants walk around it, then it's bad."

So that's how they knew. The meal was delicious. Never had a problem. Knowing how poverty stricken the village was, I declined seconds. When I returned from Honduras, I read an article about the folly of testing barracuda for ciguatera poisoning by setting a piece on an ant hill.

A slight man appeared at the door. Luis invited him in. A cousin. One of many. He ate and left. Another man appeared and did the same. Luis always had enough food for everyone.

Luis sat erect. A sign. Helena quickly got up and cleared the table. It was dark but for the single bulb over our heads. Luis disappeared and returned with a box clutched to his chest. Carefully he opened it and revealed a backgammon board carved from Honduran mahogany.

"Backgammon?" he asked.

"Sure, but I haven't played for years."

"Then it will be a cinch to beat you."

Backgammon on Guanaja is as serious as soccer. It's a board game involving moving small disks around a board and dice. It takes luck and strategy to get all the disks around and off the board. My reckless and fast playing threw Luis off, and I found myself close to winning. A quiet came over the room as Luis took a serious view of the game and his impending defeat. A veil of hot oil flowed over my head. *Heffe! What are you thinking??!!* Luis recovered without a sense of my suddenly acquired bad luck. I still won, but by a close margin that prompted Luis to throw down another challenge.

Luis played the second game fearlessly, deliberately, and without mercy. The dice turned to favor him. Double sixes on the dice came again and again. Luis finished me off. "One game each," Luis said, laughing. "Early day tomorrow. Time to head back. Our championship match will have to wait."

We felt our way into the night. The sky was speckled with thousands upon thousands of brightly twinkling stars from one end of the horizon to the other. Constellations bulged and boldly blinked through the night sky.

It took a minute for my eyes to grow accustomed to the blackness. We stepped into his boat and slowly motored past other docks, looking for one with an awaiting cousin.

"Luis, it's black as pitch out here. How can you see?"

Luis laughed. "This is my home."

No lights. Just the feel of the night to guide the way for a man who had made this trip ten thousand times.

"Why don't you have running lights?"

"It blinds my vision."

"Vision for what?"

Luis pointed to the outline of the mountains that rose out of the sea into the skies. "If all you can see is black, it has to be land. Stars light the sky. If I had running lights, I wouldn't be able to see where I was."

"What about other boats?"

"When we come this way, we stay closer to land than those going back to the village."

Lights appeared in the distance. They were harsh on our night vision and seemed rude to the moment. The Posada. They suddenly tugged me back to the world I knew. It was hard to believe how such poverty existed so close to a high-end resort.

We heard music. And laughing. A party on the beach was in full swing. I sipped a rum drink, enjoyed the music, and watched the festivities. Any other time I would have joined with vigor. But this night I felt out of place. Perhaps misaligned by my journey to Savanah Bight. Perhaps the realization of who I was and was not.

I got up at dawn to the squawking of quetzals flying through the jungle. I kissed Peri, and she climbed aboard the boat to take her to the airstrip. I never saw her again. I lost touch when she married and left her position at the Posada. I connected with old friends in Guatemala who said she sat on a dock all day reading books until she tired of it and left her absent husband.

A year passed. A new journey to the Posada. Good to return. New faces. A new batch of children turned men. Young shy girls turned brides to the once gangly boys. Luis? Not to be seen. He was on holiday the week I arrived. Perhaps he would show. He sent word from the village that he would come visit. But I left Honduras without seeing my good friend.

Months passed. Word came from friends about a boating accident on Guanaja. I contacted George Cundiff, owner of the Posada. He was a colorful man with a knack for telling stories that kept me on the edge of my seat. It was good to hear his voice.

George told me of the tragic accident between two boats. A sudden crash just around eastern Honduras from the Posada. There was the silence of motors and yelling. The surviving boat raced toward the lights of the Posada to summon help. George collected flashlights and a small army of strong young men. Fragments of wood marked the disaster. Gasoline flattened the chop. Lights darted around, frantically poking into the blackness. Alas! A body bobbing facedown, lifeless. And then another. They found a third. A man. Still alive! George pulled him into the boat. The man was semi-conscious. George placed his hand under the man's head as a cushion, only to discover it was crushed. The man's eyes locked onto George's. Nothing was spoken. He closed his eye, his body went limp, and he was gone.

"Hay uno más por aquí!" [There is one more over here!] shouted one of the searchers. Heads turned. Flashlights raced around and found a small hand holding on to a piece of wreckage. They raced to the person. A child. Scared yet miraculously unharmed.

There was silence and quivering in George's voice as he told the rest of the story. "It was Tito, Jeff. And his wife, and sister-in-law. All dead."

My soul drained as I felt the experience George described. "And the child, George?"

"Tito's daughter, Lisa. She survived."

So goes the way of the boat captain traveling in the darkness without running lights. It was his home. He knew the way too well. So did others.

I spent years traveling around Central America, learning a language that came slowly and with great difficulty, and coming to understand the culture of gentle people. I wanted to be one of them. On May 1, 1995, during my visit to Savanah Bight, I came to the realization that I could only be a visitor. And, sadly, it was the same day I abandoned my quest for fluent Spanish. It was also the last time I saw my friendly host, Luis—Tito. We still have that championship match to play.

THE EDGE OF WITS' END

DIVE LOG

Date: September 1995
Location: Grouper Gully, San Salvador, Bahamas

I drifted over the abyss and hovered at the edge of a six-thousand-foot drop. I was on a mission that smart people would tell me was foolish. I was beyond that point, and my next step could carry me down with the capsule I'd been sent to bury.

I rose early, that cool September morning a year before this trip. Not even the birds were up. Tightened my sandals and headed out for a walk. When my night kinks melted, my body got into the rhythm. The only sound was the crunching of pulverized coral under my feet. I looked to the heavens—to the east and a milky-blue sky with what was left of the previous night's moon. *Crunch. Crunch. Crunch.* I studied the moon in this morning setting and found something peaceful in its fading color. I etched the vision of it into memory. And it stayed with me for all the days that followed. *Crunch. Crunch. Crunch.*

I looked to the moon, feeling compelled to say something. "You know, I'm really not a bad person."

"No one said you were." I stopped abruptly. Early morning silence enshrouded me but for the awakening birds.

Who was talking to me? Was I going mad? It was not the moon but the source of the moon's light. It had to be.

"I thought you were punishing me."

"It is you who thinks it, not me."

"I am so lost."

"You are wandering on the path set before you."

"I thought you were gone."

"I never lost sight of you."

"What shall I do?"

"Turn around and go back. Then take your pen and write."

"Write? What shall I write?"

"You will know. Now, go back."

That voice was not mine. It was far too wise for this angry person to have spoken such gentle words. They were too understanding and too soothing for one still clutching an angry sword and seeking revenge.

I am not here to convince you of things.

The years of silence between my Maker and me ended, but our reconnection did not come with a single conversation. The road to recovery was one of steep passages, loose rocks, and a lot of backsliding.

I was not out of the woods, so goes the cliché. I had lost my job and thought it was because of incompetence, but it wasn't. I floundered. Unable to find suitable work in Arizona, I felt forced to leave my family for work in another state. I found myself in and out of bad-fit relationships that bludgeoned my soul. "Betrayal" was the song that continued to resonate in the reaches of my mind. I found myself regressing, and whatever life was left within was slowly being choked out of me. I needed help.

I sat in Dr. Henry's chair for hours, attempting to squeeze all the puss from my wounds. She told me I needed dramatic action to exorcise the hurt and pain before there could be healing. She sent me away to write about my feelings and then ceremoniously destroy what I wrote.

"I already did that, but I didn't ceremoniously destroy them."

"Then you have them. Bring them to me."

I took the pages to Dr. Henry. She scanned through them and handed them back to me. "These are not feelings. These are rationalizations. This gives others the benefit of the doubt, and you are still left with emptiness and pain. You lost your wife. You lost your job. What was once yours is now gone and can never come back. That is what you have to write about. Where does it hurt? How deep is the cut? Come back with your feelings bleeding all over the pages."

A lone lamp dimly lit the area around my typewriter, its puny light sucked dry by the surrounding darkness. Outside, an errant lightning storm zapped and cracked its angry fury on the desert floor. Raindrops rapped harshly on the windows, and sudden flashes flooded the house with blinding white light. Late into the night my fingers furiously hammered out words of anger and hurt, strange words I did not understand. It was the writing of the inner voice of a hurting soul. Rolling thunder rattled the house and punctuated the drama. Noise from the typewriter keys striking the paper sounded like bullets shot from a machine gun—each one cutting through me with the crudeness of rusty nails. Tears shot past my determination to get the job done.

Dawn arrived with air heavy from the midnight storm. It was deafeningly quiet. I found myself cast lifelessly on the floor, flanked by pages filled with newly discovered feelings. My emotions lay ragged and dismantled, clawed raw and bloody from the word battle the night before. My soul wandered in a stupor. I gaped in disbelief at the damage within. Was this part of the process? Could I be repaired? Would I ever be alive again?

"Now you're ready for a bonfire," said Dr. Henry.

Never leave a romantic in charge of a bonfire. They will do it with sentiment and flair, and make it unforgettable. The hurt had to be sent somewhere far away—far away to a distant place that would be impossible to find its way back or be found. *The abyss! Yes! The abyss! Send it into the abyss! That is both dramatic and ceremonious.*

I burned what I had written. I watched the edge of the papers turn brown and then curl as small yellow flames danced across the edges. The flames left a small field of scorched onionskin. Some words remained, yet faintly visible. I pulverized the parched ashes and transformed them to fine gray dust. I looked at the cremated remains. *So few ashes. So much pain.*

I cut a short piece of PVC pipe used for irrigation systems. This would be the vehicle to carry away the hurt. I tested it by adding and removing pebbles, capping the ends, and setting it free in the swimming pool. It seemed important to the ritual to have it sink slowly. When satisfied, I poured the ashes into the PVC pipe and glued it shut.

I was ready. I packed it away and headed for the islands for the next step, the ceremonious destruction.

***

I told Kevin, the divemaster, I had something to do. He gave me an inquisitive look.

"I'm going out there," I said as I pointed to blue water.

"You know we don't allow that".

"I'm not asking for permission. There's something I must do. You know my skill."

Kevin nodded and walked away.

I pulled the pipe from my backpack and stuffed it into the pocket of my BC. I scurried to be the first in the water.

Grouper Gully was a favored dive site in the Bahamas. It was perched at the edge of an abyss, and a marine research team once sent its aqua "geek" submersible down the wall to validate that it was a sheer six-thousand-foot drop. Even in the clearest water the depth would absorb most of the light long before the capsule hit bottom. It was the perfect place to send the demons.

I looked around as if to say my goodbyes and the glided down headfirst, making my way to the edge of the reef.

Even though my soul had not healed, and I had yet to convince myself I was trustworthy with this mission to venture into the deep, I decided as part of the ritual to monitor my depth not by my gauges, but by the sounds of my bubbles, the viscosity of my air, and vanishing color. I stuffed my dive computer into my BC so I wouldn't be tempted to check it. Placing myself in peril was a necessary part of this journey.

I swam away from the wall until it became a shadow, and then it vanished in the cerulean openness.

I could hear my heart. I could feel the air swirling around in my lungs. It felt syrupy as I sucked it in. I could feel the depth pressing against my chest. My bubbles crackled. I knew I was at eighty feet when the dark shadows of narcosis drifted across my view. I continued to descend. Focusing became more difficult. I felt as if I were standing at cliff's edge and below was a great flow of molten lava. I descended past one hundred feet and found myself surrounded in gray blueness. No up. No down. No anything. All orientation was gone except knowing that bubbles went up.

I hovered. There was nothing to protect me now but my tenacity to hold an awareness of my surroundings as narcosis tried changing my plan. Its lure to the deep was tempting. I fought to stay alert to the depth by the sound of my bubbles and sensitivity to pressure changes in my ears. The conniving demons were still alive in the capsule. I could feel them. I lost the awareness of time. Why had I chosen to come here, to a place where all that wisdom dictates is foolishness?

I was in harm's way.

I heard a voice telling me to slip deeper. Was it my death wish, demon trickery, or did the voice come from my Maker?

Aloneness pervaded. A change in pressure told me I was sinking. Until the capsule was gone, the ceremony commanded that I not refer to my gauges. Maintaining control became more difficult as my emotions and fears began bouncing off one another, throwing me further and further out of balance and distracting my awareness.

Suddenly I realized I was lost. I was in danger. But narcosis dulled my fear while my experience kept telling me to finish my business and go shallow. I was intoxicated. I looked around, knowing that I might not be going back after all. I was there—there at my wits' end. I drifted into the last battlefield with my demons. They were pulverized ashes, but they were still alive—still beating to get out of the capsule.

I looked around at the nothingness below, and recited the short speech I had memorized for this moment:

"In this capsule are the remains of years of resentment and hurt. You demons are locked inside. The abyss will carry you away. When the blue of the deep obscures my sight of you, I shall be free to regain the power I gave away. When you land six thousand feet below, you will be out of my reach. And I will be out of yours. When I swim back over the top of the reef, I will be done with you forever."

I looked at the capsule, almost reluctant to release it.

"Let it go." A calming voice filled my head.

I was not alone as I thought.

I looked at the capsule, ignoring the voice.

"Let go of the hurt," came a soft voice.

I opened my hand and let the capsule go.

As I watched it drift away, I felt an urge to swim down after it. After all, I did not deserve a good life. It was the snap of the demons' whip—a deception to take me with them. They were still in control. Had I obeyed, it would have been suicidal.

"Let it go. You have more days. Your job here is done. Go back."

I looked around and headed eastward. Soon the wall came through the blue and took shape. I swam over the edge of the reef and joined other divers under the boat. I hung on the tethered line for a long safety stop. Mission accomplished. I was overwhelmed with a sense of relief.

Back on board, Kevin looked toward me and nodded as he took note of my safe return. I sat quietly and waited for the next dive.

Anyone who dives will tell you my actions were reckless. But this was not a mission of personal responsibility. Rather, it was one to take a stand against the desperation that had made my life an insufferable existence. Demons are like the thugs that show up in your store demanding a 20 percent cut of your weekly receipts as insurance to protect you from other thugs. Over time, they will strip you of your dignity and turn you into a coward. At times we must place ourselves in harm's way to put an end to those who seek to destroy us. When I dropped the capsule and let go of my past, I could start to rebuild my life.

LISA'S SECRET PROFESSION

DIVE LOG

Date: May 1996
Location: Ruthie "C" Dock Dive, Guanaja, Honduras

Lisa refused to reveal her profession and preferred to keep her thoughts to herself. She was an enigma. Communicating with her felt like a game of twenty questions. Along the way she became glued to my side, and it was like trying to shake a wet potato peeling off my hand. But when I said goodbye to her, I wished I didn't have to.

Lisa and Peri arrived on the island the same day I did. I had known Peri for ten years, but Lisa was a new face. As Peri and I attempted to reconnect, Lisa, the quiet wallflower, sat nearby, watching without expression and listening without reaction. She neither smiled nor frowned. At first I thought she was being polite, but then I began wondering if she was annoyed with me for interfering with her holiday with Peri.

As a scuba instructor, I watched other divers to size up their skill, experience, and comfort. I wondered how Lisa had gotten her certification. Perhaps she was merely "rusty" from years of not diving. She came across as being inept and proud of it. She laughed at her novice moves, walked to the dive platform of the rocking boat with fins already on, and held up other divers when she realized she had left her mask behind. I avoided her by rolling over the side, but the calamity of Lisa continued underwater. She flailed, propelled herself with her arms while allowing her legs to drag, and constantly added and released air from her BC to control her buoyancy. She appeared oblivious to her underwater surroundings. This all could have been resolved with a one-dive refresher, but I was not going to suggest it or become involved in a rescue mission.

Peri left the island early in the week. Lisa looked around for another dive buddy. I spent half a day turning away whenever she looked toward me. During cocktail hour, I ducked and avoided eye contact. I enjoyed diving with different people, but Lisa would never be on my list. I relaxed when I saw the back of her head as she talked to another diver on the other side of the bar, but suddenly, she appeared in my face. "Can I buddy up with you?"

I hesitated, looked away, and scratched my eyebrow.

"I don't know anyone else to ask. I won't be a burden. I promise. Please."

I looked into her puppy-dog eyes, sighed deeply, and slowly shook my head, thinking, *Why me?* "Very well," I said. Call me soft.

***

As a diving buddy, it is difficult *not* to get to know something about the other person. Introductions usually include asking who you are, where you're from, and what you do. Yes, these are good icebreaker questions, but over time I had difficulty with them, because it seemed like many people attempted to align themselves with others who were dripping with titles, trophies, and success stories. What pushed me over the edge was the time I watched a diver approach a man and ask him about his profession. When he told her he was a house painter, she looked scornful and walked away. A person's work history was not part of my repertoire of pre-dive questions, but I did want to know about my buddy's diving experiences.

I could never understand why some people placed so much emphasis on a person's occupation. It annoyed me so much that I conjured up job descriptions to elicit something other than "Oh, that's nice." I was a brain surgeon, an automobile repossession thug, and a mercenary in Nicaragua, and named other offbeat career paths to fit my whim of the moment. On one occasion I told someone I was a drug runner from Central America in search of a new route to the States. Shortly after that an overly friendly stranger with an Oklahoma twang strolled up to me. "Howdy, neighbor, how ya doin'? I'm a chicken salesman. Whadda you do?" A chicken salesman in Honduras? Right. And why are you telling me this? A few days later the chicken salesman and his team arrested some smugglers and confiscated a nice-looking fast boat. Somebody had told on me. I had become a suspect. I immediately resorted to owning up to "being into computers" and never indulged in such foolish antics again.

* * *

Lisa was noticeably reserved when it came to name, rank, and serial number kinds of questions. When asked, she evaded with "Oh, I own a business." The more people persisted and pressed, the more aloof she became. I became exasperated with the plethora of meddlers. Her demeanor piqued my curiosity, but to inquire would have been invasive and put me on the same plane as those whose poor behavior I despised. If she wanted me to know, she would tell me in her own good time.

Lisa seemed to mix well with other women but was standoffish around men. Bad history? An ugly experience? Something else? She was cute and mysterious, and—except for diving with her—I found her attractive and wanted to talk about something else besides diving. Until the neon "keep back, buster" sign on her forehead fell off, she was off-limits.

After the afternoon dive, Lisa invited me to make the killer hike to the tallest and steepest mountain on the island. I'd never done it before and agreed to accompany her. It was one of those activities that you do once to say you've done it. The climb was long and challenging. Many of the slopes were so steep and slippery with wet leaves that climbing would have been impossible without the help of jungle vines. As we approached the top, she insisted I lead. The sun became a late-afternoon haze as it got closer to the horizon. Still, it was hot and sultry. I looked back for Lisa. She had shed her sweat-filled shirt. She smiled, shrugged, and said, "Hey, it's hot. A girl's gotta do what a girl's gotta do."

We stood at the top, looking out over the island, the fringe reef and cays, and the calming ocean. Lisa looked out at the horizon and said, "What do you do?"

"Like in my work?"

"Yeah."

"I head up an information technology department for a city in Arizona."

She asked nonstop and probing questions about what that meant and the kind of work such a job entailed. She was the first person in all my journeys to appear genuinely interested in my background beyond my job title.

Finally we stood quietly looking out at the landscape.

"OK, I'll tell you what I do," she said.

I nodded casually and kept my eyes out to sea.

"I own my condominium free and clear. I have a staff of twelve employees. And… I drive a paid-for BMW."

"Impressive. So what kind of work do you do?"

"You'll probably laugh at me when I tell you."

"Why would I do that?"

"Well, if you knew what I did, you'd probably look at me as some second-class person."

"A second-class person driving a BMW who owns her own condo free and clear? Why would someone think that makes you second-class?"

"Because of what I do."

"OK, kid, quit dancing. What do you do?"

"I own a cleaning business. I clean houses."

"And you think that's second-class?"

"I don't, but others might."

"So this is why you've been tight-lipped when asked what you do."

"You've been spying on me?"

"It's obvious with the way you duck the question. It's amusing. You're embarrassed about your profession, aren't you?"

"I just don't want people judging me even though I am successful at what I do."

"This explains things. And that's why you told me you drive a BMW and live in a paid-for condo but nothing about your profession. What's the rest of your story?"

"I clean villas. I keep them clean even when the owners are away. They call me when they plan to bring company and I get their places ready—like making up beds and setting out towels and flowers and a fruit bowl. With twelve employees, I seldom do the cleaning. I do the bookkeeping, scheduling, coordinating, meeting new clients. That sort of thing."

"And you think that's a lowly profession?"

"Like I said, I don't, but many do."

"I'm guessing your clients give you the keys to those villas so you can come and go as you're needed."

Lisa shrugged. "Yeah, so?"

"Lisa, you're not a cleaning lady. You're a business-minded professional who knows the essentials of integrity, dependability, and what it takes to earn and protect your credentials. Those qualities are rare and hard to come by. I'm sure clients appreciate and pay you well for your high standards. That's how you get paid-for condos and BMWs."

Lisa looked out over the sea. "Wow! You're right! I never looked at it like that."

"And I'll bet you don't even have to advertise, do you? Your new clients all come from referrals, right?"

Lisa nodded. "I just want to be accepted as the person I am, not judged by my seemingly unsophisticated and lowly profession. When I told others what I did, most of them saw me swaying mops on floors and feather dusters on menageries."

"Maybe you should work on your job title. You know, kinda like rebranding? Now, don't get me wrong for this comparison. It worked for the garbage men in New York City when they became sanitation engineers. They got more respect, and some were being paid eighty thousand dollars just for picking up people's trash and throwing cans around in an alley. We could have fun dreaming up different job titles for you, and maybe you won't feel the need to keep your profession a secret. But right now the sun's getting low, and we have a slippery mountain to slide down."

***

Whoever she was, Lisa had a good sense of humor and was willing to try anything, but she remained an unaware diver, and that made her a liability. She told me she sought me out as a dive buddy because I looked like I knew what I was doing. Rats! And here I thought it was my charm and good looks.

***

The *Ruthie "C"* was a small wooden powerboat resting in forty-five feet of water fifty yards off the main dock. She was not a five-star attraction, but an easy late afternoon dive. Visibility was predictably poor—*Ruthie "C"* sat in a never-ending brownish fog. She made a good reef; fish flocked to her. They seemed less skittish around divers in the poor visibility.

A line fastened to one of the dock piles led out into the cloudy obscurity, and at the other end was *Ruthie "C."* In the outbound journey, we passed over a bottom of soft sand forming small hills and valleys, tall seagrass, discarded tires, and jellyfish undulating upside down on the sand. Five minutes of finning got us to the sunken boat.

Another line tied to the bow was attached to an orange surface buoy to mark the vessel's location. She was in a boat channel. Divers had to be wary if they surfaced or they risked getting whacked by a propeller. The murky environment, its stillness, the silenced sound, and the tepid water gave a sense of being closed in. This was a bland dive. Did not attract many divers. But there was something eerie and mysterious about this place that lured me to it.

My instructor background gave me the tendency to point out camouflaged sea life. Lisa seemed to enjoy the experience and studied everything in great detail. She was unafraid to hold what I handed her, and she was vigilant about placing everything back in its home.

We checked gauges. Time to head back.

Lisa had enough air to check out the fish and other critters congregating under the dock. But she was having difficulty staying down, because we were in shallow water, and tanks tend to float up when light on air. We compensate by proper weighting and breathing techniques, a skill Lisa had yet to learn.

Lisa constantly floated toward the surface and struggled to get back down. An outstretched hand beckoned for help. I swam to her and pulled her down, and soon she was right back up there, flailing with an outstretched hand. I could see going through this a few times, but she was becoming irritating.

We were still in a boat lane, not a good place to have buoyancy issues. I collected a few discarded conch shells that would make good temporary weights. When I looked back for her, time stood still. I watched in horror as a small outboard boat headed for the dock, Lisa in its path, unaware. I lunged toward her in what felt like slow motion. I pulled on her gear, convinced she was about to be hit by the boat and carved up by the propeller. Yanking her down pulled me up. I rolled over on top of her and ducked my head just as the boat passed over us. *CLANK, CLANK!* The propeller struck my tank.

My imagination went wild. All I could see was Lisa's brains strewn all over the bottom and fish swooping in to help with the cleanup. Imagine that: fish cleaning up after the cleaning lady.

I pushed Lisa down and under the pier toward safety. We swam to the exit steps and surfaced, expecting to find the boaters looking around for what they had hit. We were alone on the dock.

"Didn't you hear that boat?"

"No."

"Then you don't know it almost ran over you?"

"So that's why you jerked at my BC and pulled me down." She looked over at the boat with her hands over her mouth, then thrust her arms around my neck yelling, "My hero. My hero! You saved my life!"

I didn't see it that way, but it was the first sign of any emotion I had seen from her all week.

***

Evening ended and so ended my stroll down to the dock where Lisa had almost left her brains the day before. The next day was going-home day, and it was my ritual to visit places, remember the moments, thank my Lord for a safe trip, and, of course, have a conversation with my friend the moon. Moonbeams on the water and a warm breeze wrote the postscripts that kept me coming back here over the years. I took one last look before closing my door and ending another chapter.

Tap, tap, tap. I awoke to a knocking at my neighbor's door. It kept up. I heard soft singing. Got up to take a look. Opened the louvers on the door. A visitor… not next door, but at mine. When I opened the door, I found Lisa swaying rhythmically while singing a soft song.

"I'm soaking wet and it's getting cold out here." With a quick flick of her arms she discarded her T-shirt. She brushed past me. I closed the door. Arms flowed around my neck as she swayed and sang. Yikes! I was being seduced!

I had never before been loved so gently and with such potency. Two people lay listlessly in the jungle mist as the ceiling fan moaned and cooled sensitive bodies recovering from the stolen moment.

Lisa walked to the window and opened the louvers. She was a sinuous shadow as the moonlight traced blue-white lines around her silhouette. She turned, drew close, and whispered, "You saved my life. Thank you. And thank you for being so patient with me. I shall remember you always."

She opened the door, picked up her shirt, and vanished amidst the night sounds of the Honduran jungle.

* * *

The quetzal birds screeched in the early dawn. Their sounds echoed and ricocheted off the morning dew to awaken the sleeping jungle. They do it every day... my wake-up call. But this dawn... it was time to go home.

And Lisa? I never saw or heard from her again.

What is it about the islands that causes people to find themselves hopelessly lost in its enchantment while tasting life's delicious red strawberries? What is the intoxication that lures a person to tease the intimacy of touch and recklessly embrace discarded inhibition?

How sad it is that we put the islands, the romance, the fantasies, and the memories aside and then return to a place that we work so hard to escape.

MY DEAR FRIEND THE MOON

DIVE LOG

Date: August 1996
Location: Vicky's Reef, San Salvador, Bahamas

When I turned on the flashlight, I could see. When I turned it off, I could see further, the world came to me, and the moon made everything safe.

The moon lit the white sandy sea floor like fluorescent lights in a workshop. That night I didn't need flashlights in the shallow sand at the edge of the reef. Nearby I could see a cluster of divers and lights darting wildly in search of something to see. The vexing noise of bubbles rumbled their way to the surface. I fled from the glow of their lights and found a faraway place where I could be alone.

I turned out my light and lay back in the sand—just me and the nocturnal sea. My breathing slowed, and small bubbles reflected the sparkles from the moon as they drifted slowly toward the surface. I looked to the moon. Its brilliance was almost too much for my eyes. *Hello, my friend, how are you tonight?*

A shadow approached. The creature hovered close to the bottom. I propped up on my elbows as it headed straight toward me. A large southern stingray with a marauding bar jack was out to dine and unconcerned about my presence. I sat motionless. It bumped my leg, dug down into the sand looking for precious morsels, then turned and continued its search in another direction.

I relaxed in the privilege of my brief visit. We are intruders down there. The fish inhabitants usually leave the neighborhood when divers thunder into town. Mr. Stingray ignored me. I was no threat. I found myself in a place in the sea I always wanted to be. I had finally been accepted by Planet Ocean.

Another silhouette appeared in the distance. Barracuda or shark? Too far to tell. I don't like darting fish—especially big ones. It means they are aggravated or hungry. Better keep an eye on this one. It vanished behind a coral ridge. I turned my attention back to the bright moon. Got lost in the honor of the moment and the solace of weightlessness. The sand was still warm from the radiant energy of the day.

SWISH! A darting silhouette flew over me and vanished before I had a chance to react. I righted myself on the sand—propped up on my knees. *SWISH!* It made another pass from behind. Reef shark! My restive moment ended. This guy was checking me out! If it had wanted to take a taste, it would have nibbled by now. It did not swim back and forth with tight, jerky movements. Its pectoral fins were not pointed down, and it did not curve its back. The shark did not have the behavior I was taught to avoid.

Before I became too comfortable in thinking it was all clear, I wondered if I were pushing my luck. I recalled the question about sharks on my basic open water certification exam—they are unpredictable. Discomfort tested my temptation to turn on my light. You know, we did this as children to send the snakes back under the bed. But I could see more without the light, and it was doubtful that a puny flashlight would thwart the big guy looking over the dinner menu.

After its menacing passes, the shark left. *Should I retreat to the safety of blasting lights and annoying divers?* I decided to take my chances where I was. I sank back to the bottom and gazed up at the moon. Breathing resumed its peaceful pattern. Although I seldom think about Planet Earth while diving, the brilliance of the moonlight sent my thoughts to reflect on how the moon came to mean so much to me. It had become my companion to soothe and light my darkness. It followed without talk like a guardian secretly sent by the family to protect me. When the phase of the moon made it impossible to see, it vanished like a servant going home to report to the master. I searched the evening sky for the sliver of the new moon. When I found it at sundown in the western sky, all was well with the world. *Hello, my friend. It's nice to see you again.*

As the years took the sharpness from my eyes, the vivid face of the moon vanished, and its edges turned soft. But its light was forever loyal. Always reliable. Always lighting my way during the long nights of bitter weeping that drained me for days. Always lighting the night while I talked to myself. My friend the moon. Never judging. Never telling. Just comforting a hurting heart. After a while I began talking to it. Or was I praying? But my moon friend simply sat up there in the night sky, warming me with its smile, and handing me messages from my Maker.

* * *

The cluster of dive lights stirred me out of my reflection. I checked my gauges and bottom time. Down fifty minutes. Time to head to the surface. I swam toward the boat. Its black silhouette and strobe marked its location. I looked one last time at the moon and floated to the surface.

Night diving is a thrilling experience for most divers. There always seems to be more buzzing on deck after night dives than those made in daylight. That night, people took to their groups and talked about lobsters, sea anemones, moray eels, crabs, turtles, and octopuses. I sat alone, quietly looking at the moon as we headed back to the marina.

In this world we believe what we believe. We see what we want to create. We wear filters to temper our perceptions. This explains all the omnipresent diversity that makes us all the same through our uniqueness.

Hello, my dear friend the moon. You are my guiding light sent by my Maker to light my path until I find my way back home.

SHADOWS IN THE SEA

TRAVEL JOURNAL

Date: August 1997
Location: San Salvador, Bahamas

I spotted it drifting south with the tide. How it remained afloat was a mystery. I swam to save it from a sad destiny. My noble mission jeopardized my own safety. In the process of rescuing it, could it have been what rescued me? To reward me for my gallant effort, I found a shadow in the sea and momentary companionship—the kind you want to last forever.

Nine of us crowded into the twin engine plane. I sat on the left to get a good aerial view of the inn as we took off. The small plane charged the runway and quickly became a vanishing speck to those waving us off. We banked hard and headed back over the island toward the States.

Down below, the inn went about its lazy ways in the Bahamas sunshine. The nearby beach was spotless—cleaned just a few days ago by powerful waves sent by a distant tropical storm. The beach was barren except for a weather-beaten lounge chair half buried in the sand.

I pressed my fingers to the window and whispered, "Goodbye, good friend."

* * *

New trips always bring the excitement of anticipation, new friends, new experiences, new discoveries. I had no one with me to share the romantic ambience of this magical paradise, so it was doubtful this trip could have ranked among my most memorable.

I had come talk to my soul, listen to what my Maker had to say, bask in sunsets, sing to the moon, wish for mermaids. It was quite a list of hopefuls.

Late afternoon brought its own personality. Sky colors softened. The sea flattened and the wind gave way to a gentle breeze. The sun became a warming honey yellow and enlarged as it drifted toward the horizon. The colors of the sea blended—pale in contrast to the brilliance of the sun on the golden sandy stretch of beach.

How should one spend these moments? I pictured a mate. One who loved the ambience and was eager to become lost in the same passion. Could such a person exist anymore?

I glanced down the beach. A couple tossed clothing and dashed waist-deep into the water. They embraced as romantic indulgence swept them away.

To the right, a dive group from Baltimore formed a circle as they socialized, laughed, and exchanged stories. An old woman sipped a drink as she floated nearby on an inner tube tethered to a bearded man.

I waded into the water and could feel the same magic that absorbed the couple down the beach. I stretched my arms and sailed like a glider in the attitudes of soft air and silence. Even alone, it was taking me.

Along the shoreline appeared a woman. She had a girlish face—one that teases and seduces at the same time. She approached slowly with purpose and grace. Her walk was melodic. She stopped, shaded her eyes from the millions of glistening sunbeams ricocheting off the water, and looked directly toward me. She smiled and continued her walk. I watched as she disappeared down the beach.

The sun drifted farther down and kissed the world before retiring for the evening. I prepared for dinner, found an untaken seat, engaged in pleasant conversation, ate, excused myself so as not to intrude, returned to my silent room, thanked my Maker for the day, and turned out the lights.

A new day came with its constant intoxicating call of late afternoon. How it beckons. I gazed out over the blue. The Baltimore group resumed its afternoon social circle in the shallows with the old woman drifting around on the tethered inner tube. How I would have liked to have joined them, but I thought it rude to simply invite myself.

I spotted something barely afloat near the breakwater to the marina. I walked south to get a better look. A lounge chair? Got to retrieve it. Was it worth the rescue? Would vanishing without notice be the same as dying without purpose? Yes, the rescue was worthwhile. But… it was only a chair.

As I swam toward it, wind pushed it farther away—drifting farther from my reach. It was plain that in my quest to rescue a chair I was placing myself in danger. I was never a strong swimmer. *What the hell am I doing way out here? Am I here to rescue a chair or is the chair there to lure me to my doom? Who would know if I never returned?*

I should have abandoned the mission, but I was closer to the chair than to shore. A floating chair could buoy me up. I reached it moments before it would have been swept away by the outgoing tide from the marina. Slowly I worked my way against the longshore current until I felt the sand brush my toes.

I dragged the chair up onto the beach and plopped myself into it to catch my breath as I questioned the sanity of my foolishness. Maybe someone had set it adrift to end its misery. It had broken and bent parts, and missing straps. It sat cockeyed in the sand. But that afternoon I was its knight in shining armor. Or maybe we saved each other.

A new day brought dead flat seas. A tropical storm lurked at our backs, but today was beautiful. Hardly a wave in sight. The broken lounge chair—friend of none—just sat there, betrayed by uselessness and disrepair. The outgoing tide had left it half buried in sand. Certainly it would be there all week for me. Who wants broken and worthless things? I walked over to its dilapidated body, looked down at it, sighed, and whispered, "Need a friend, chair? Why am I standing here talking to a chair?"

Darkness came and brought the golden glow of the August moon. I found my friend and relaxed in its broken arms and legs. It cradled me as I watched the quiet night sky. The moon washed the sand with glistening moonbeams. A soft breeze whispered in my ears. Small clouds danced around the moon. I felt lucky to be alive and there with my two friends, the moon and an abandoned chair.

A woman approached along the shoreline, kicking the water as she moved. She looked like she could have been the one who had passed the day before. She stopped, making herself a silhouette in the moonbeams. She faced the sea and stretched her arms high over her head. Her dress swayed in the breeze. Who was this silhouette here in the cleansing breath of the night? Why did she stop there? Did she not know I was sitting close by?

She turned, walked toward me, and stopped by my side. I sat up. Confused. Why me? The evening breeze blew her hair to one side. She stood back, and with graceful moves, she slid her delicate covering over her head and dropped it in the sand. She cloaked her nakedness in the security of a trust she could not possibly have known. Her sensuous grace was alluring. She took my hand and pulled me into the sea.

Was she real or was I hallucinating and longing for the one whose ashes I had spread in Tilloo? Could it be a well-crafted dream made to look real? She was a shadow in the sea.

Moonbeams glistened on her skin. I surrendered to her arms. In the coolness of the water two became one. We drifted in weightlessness and freedom. Intimacy created privacy. The world was ours. We wrote stories—saying things without ever uttering a word.

Who was this person who had taken me? She had no voice. Only in her actions was there to be found a story. The way she approached. Her rhythmic walk. Her eyes that told me what to do. The softness of her skin. Her trust. How thoroughly the touch of her look captured my heart.

I glanced to the moon, and then back to my nameless lover. "Stay here a moment," instructed her eyes. She waded toward shore. An errant cloud suddenly whisked across the moon and turned off its romantic beams. The sky and the sea blackened. When the moon reappeared, she was gone.

The late-night romantic lady vanished with the same mysteriousness as she had appeared. Was she just a muse? Had I strayed into a dream? How frightfully real she seemed. *What has taken over me?* I walked back to my lounge chair and found my shirt folded and carefully placed on the seat and crowned with a small seashell.

On my last night on the island, the late-night moon brought its beams dancing on the water. I sat in the chair. Waiting. Waiting. Waiting for her. I felt only the soft breeze and the hush of the waves tickling my toes. She did not come.

I had come to the island to find answers to tough questions and words for a fading song. There were no answers and no stories to write except for my abandoned chair and the mysterious lady who took me into the sea.

How we complicate our lives with so much that has so little meaning. I go to this place, relax, spend a week being someone and somewhere I wish I could always be, and then "go back to reality." Maybe it is on those islands that who we become is nothing more than who we are without the constant pressure of the clock. Perhaps this is the world we are destined to know.

* * *

The drone of the airplane brought me back. I looked down to the beach for a last glimpse of the week just passed. Gone were the coral rocks and coconuts that had come for a brief visit and been swept clean by the storm surge of the wayward hurricane. Gone all but an old, abandoned and broken lounge chair anchored solidly in the sand. Waiting alone. Waiting for a new companion. *Goodbye, good friend.*

SMALL SHELL FROM THE SEA

Small shell from the sea,
From where have you come?
What path carried you gently to my fingers?
How far away is the life you once held?

Small shell from the sea,
You made your sacred journey home.
Tell me you're here.
Etch me a memory and whisper quiet love songs.
Sing in the moon and dance on moonbeams.

Small shell from the sea.
I cry at night.
I'm far away and so bitterly alone.
Waiting, waiting, waiting for her return.
She was just a dream, just a pretend
But for a shell she left behind.

Small shell from the sea,
Carry me close to her bosom
In the warmth of her tender love.
She is never far, only a heartbeat away.
Hear my whisper—telling of gentleness that awaits
When I can be with her again.

INDEPENDENCE DAY

TRAVEL JOURNAL

Date: July 10, 1998
Location: San Salvador Island, Bahamas

On this date, twenty-five years before, the Bahamas became a free and sovereign country, ending 325 years of British rule. I mingled with a friendly community, eager to share their holiday and food, but fried chicken will never be the same.

Bruce was a Bahamian local and captain of our dive boat. His invitation to his settlement for a holiday lunch celebration was an honor. It was Independence Day in the Bahamas, and the entire island was alive with merriment.

Children scampered about with the excitement you would find on Christmas Day. A small, thin boy approached with a red cape tied around his neck, proclaiming to be Superman. His smile was broad, and it seemed impossible that he could have so many teeth except for the few missing in the front. He flexed his muscles and bolted off to the dock. By the time I had caught up to watch, he had already scurried back for another ten-foot plunge. He once again flexed his toothpick arms and rushed to fly off the dock into a pile of rocks below. My warning to wait was wasted. His leap went into slow motion as I put my hands to my mouth, knowing I was about to witness a tragic event. Moments before the collision, a large wave broke, caught him, and whisked him to safety. *Was I the only one who seemed to be concerned?*

Superman had protection from an army of angels. All across the island were children, exuding zest and energy, who somehow managed to avoid catastrophe. There were no hospitals on the island—just clinics that could patch scratches and apply a splint to a broken arm. Bashed heads required medical treatment from skilled people almost two hundred miles away in Nassau. To see all this energy running around so recklessly gave me more evidence that there had to be a God. If confronted by disbelievers demanding proof, all I would need to do is point to that small settlement on San Salvador.

Bruce yelled to get my attention and waved at me to come into the church. Tables were loaded with platters of fish, chicken, rice, and beans. Women stood behind the tables. They wore plain cotton dresses and white aprons and gave large smiles as they thanked me for coming. Very Bahamian. They asked if I preferred chicken or fish. "Chicken," I said. They handed me a paper plate loaded with chicken on a bed of rice and beans.

I found a rickety stool near a wooden hut partially roofed by dried palm fronds blowing in the wind. Locals propped themselves on the stools as crossed arms kept their chins off the sunbaked tabletop. They watched with faceless expressions and bloodshot eyes. It was plain they were struggling with too much rum under the midday sun.

I smiled and said, "Hello." They gave me blank looks and watched as I took a bite of their food. It was awful! The chicken tasted more like old fish cooked in cheap oil than it did like chicken. It was overcooked and tastelessly crunched in my mouth. Chicken bones splintered. How could I spit it out without dishonoring my hosts?

The inebriated men sat watching me as they wobbled and bobbed on the stools. I wondered how many of me they saw. I figured I was too blurry for them to notice what I needed to do. They said nothing as I discreetly spit the bones into my hand and then flung them into the sand. I turned the piece over in search of real meat. That is when I discovered the other eye to the fish head I had just tried to eat.

THE MYSTERIOUS MR. FORBES

TRAVEL JOURNAL

Date: July 1998
Location: San Salvador Island, Bahamas

No afternoon dive today. Resting up for the night dive. Mr. Forbes pulled up in the van and opened the doors, waiting for riders. In respect, I jumped aboard and prepared myself to see the same thing I had seen many times before.

He was a San Salvador Island icon. Children flocked around and feared him at the same time. One day he disappeared, as will happen to us all. I see a man who wore his cap slightly cocked. It looked like it had caught a limb of a passing tree, but he never bothered to straighten it.

He was tall, pure jet-black Bahamian, and appeared unconcerned and unfriendly. His dark eyes warned others not to trespass. They looked suspiciously for tricksters, who may have thought his lack of education translated into a stupid person. He was a private man. Over the years that I knew him, he looked right through me as we passed, and he never gave me any more attention than a glance.

The dive resort offered three dives daily. A night dive on Tuesday freed up the afternoon for napping, exploring, bicycling, scootering, or other activities.

Mr. Forbes pulled up in a van for an island tour. I had been on it several times over the years, so there wasn't much new to discover. He waited for tour takers, and none showed up. What the hell. What's one more tour? I jumped into the van.

"Come sit with me in the front."

Those were the first words Mr. Forbes uttered to me in fifteen years of diving on San Salvador. We drove to Cockburn Town and stopped at the local grocery for cold drinks. Visiting the local store was on the tour route. Mr. Forbes then drove down a dirt road I had never been on. He stopped and looked ahead. To the left was a row of weather-beaten shanties with dark screened-in porches for mosquito protection. Across the road in front of us was the edge of one of the inland ponds that form part of a great maze within the island. Mangrove trees populated the shoreline with occasional openings where I could see the pond. Along the shore were retired skiffs turned upside down and wasting away. Nearby was a no-longer-functioning rickety dock made from crooked sticks and junk-pile lumber that stood as a reminder of bygone days. Reeds protruded out of the mucky shore, old bottles and trash intertwined among them. The air was breezy and cooled by the shade trees.

Why are we stopping here? Don't you dare ask! You'll know in good time.

Mr. Forbes pointed to one of the shanties. "See dat ole house? Dat was my mama's. Dat's where I grew up. See da one next to it? Dat's where I live."

"Is your mama still here?"

"She passed."

"Do you have any brothers or sisters?"

"No, they be gone, too."

"Did they live in one of these houses?"

"My brother lived in dat one and my sister lived in da one way down yonder."

"So you're all alone down here now, aren't you?"

Mr. Forbes said nothing but stared at what used to be where his mama lived. He shifted his eyes to the old dock. "When I was a boy, I brung kerosene drums from dat ole dock to the lighthouse. Back then, it only took a week. When I got to the lighthouse, I had to roll the drums up the hill to the fill tank. Then I'd bring the empty ones back."

"I've seen the island from the air. The inland waterways form a maze. How did you know your way?"

"I learnt it from my daddy. For a while, I was the only one besides him that knew da way."

"You shoved off from that dock, eh?"

"Yep. It's no good no more. I 'spect it would break up if someone was to walk on it."

"Whatever became of your father?"

"Daddy got killed in a storm."

Mr. Forbes peeled back the onion layers of his past. Ferrying kerosene back and forth to the lighthouse was his job as a boy, and his journey to manhood. It was a well-earned badge.

Continuing on with our tour, we found ourselves at the lighthouse, and it had taken us only thirty minutes to get there from the rickety dock.

I never knew why Mr. Forbes drove down that dirt road and shared his story after wordless years between us. It was a privilege to be allowed behind his curtain of privacy.

The next morning Mr. Forbes walked through the dining room of the resort carrying water for coffee. I stood by his side while he made it. He looked at me and said nothing, not even with his eyes. There was never a word spoken between us again.

Sometimes the connection with others is meant to last only a moment, at least that's how I reckoned with it. I asked myself, *What was that all about?* and concluded I wasn't supposed to know. Along the way people wandered across my path, said something that was very appropriate for the moment, and then vanished. I call them "angels," sent by God in this interwoven universe to encourage others. And it doesn't take much to become one. All we gotta do is say something kind to everyone, and maybe just one of those kind words will work magic for someone needing magic at that instant.

THE WOODEN BOAT FROM HAITI

DIVE LOG

Date: July 1998
Location: San Salvador Island, Bahamas

A small boat lay mysteriously alone on the bottom, its broken mast still jagged where it had split but had been spliced by rope in a hurry. Torn remnants of canvas told of storms and an angry Mother Nature. A wooden tiller balanced precariously in its hinge on the transom. She sat there on her side with untold secrets. Cause of death... unattended leaking.

Haitian refugees miraculously kept it afloat long enough for an ocean crossing. Immigration officials sent them home, and the boat sank as they dragged it away. A curled rope with its bitter end swayed back and forth in the surge. Bottles in a wooden box gave hints of their passage now lost in the deep.

When refugees flee a country, they usually overload their escape boat, and that places them in extreme peril even in the calmest of conditions. How many people and how many stories did that small boat carry for 315 miles without compass or chart? Perhaps they followed the North Star. What tyrannical forces or irredeemable living conditions pushed them to brave a trip that they knew could bring about a terrible death by drowning as they listened to their boatmates scream for help that could never come? What was the depth of their dedication to family that they would risk their lives hoping to find something better for loved ones? How desperate do you have be to leave your home and everything behind and make such a dangerous journey, with no assurance of the outcome?

I emerged from the dive filled with questions about the human side of the refugees' passage. Who were they? How many? What became of them? No one knew.

A year later, storm surge picked up the boat and cast it over the edge of the reef. Gone was the boat, and gone were the many stories of courage of those people taking drastic measures for drastic situations.

ORBIT'S CANYON

DIVE LOG

Date: August 2003
Location: Orbit's Canyon, San Salvador, Bahamas

I was the first human to visit this place… ever. In 1988 we found it by accident and marked its location by triangulating from objects on land. Sadly, it took only fifteen years to erase the truth and rewrite history.

The boat approached the dive site. I looked to the shoreline and checked the boat's alignment with the landmarks. We had arrived at Orbit's Canyon. This was one of my most favorite of favorites. The divemaster went forward to secure the line on the mooring ball. Engine stopped. Briefing began. "Here we are at a site called Avalanche."

Avalanche!!?? Avalanche, my ass! This is not Avalanche! This is Orbit's Canyon. I corrected the divemaster. He pointed to the name on the mooring ball. We were at "Avalanche." The mooring ball said so.

Was I dreaming? Were my bearings wrong? Maybe the landmarks had changed. Maybe this wasn't Orbit's Canyon. My mind drifted into the archives of my past, trying to recall the directions being sent from those days gone by.

***

In 1988, Rich and Nancy Norton brought a group from Connecticut to dive on San Salvador Island. With nine people, theirs was the largest group there that week, and the Riding Rock Inn was full at fifteen guests. Rich's group was honest, sincere, and uncomplicated. They took things at face value and were quick to have a good time. I was lucky to have been assigned to the *San Sally*—the boat also assigned to Rich's group. They quickly adopted me.

Colin, our divemaster, was a legend throughout the Bahamas. He was Bahaman born with blue eyes and blond hair, and well educated in English. His pre-dive briefings were crisp yet thorough. He treated guests as mature divers, and everyone acted that way.

Rich asked Colin to take us to a place where no one had been before. Colin scratched his chin and told us we could head south along the reef, drift slowly attached to a line, and see what we could see. It would take some patience to find a place that would be worth the exhilaration of a "virgin dive spot."

Colin jumped into the water and held a line tied to the boat. He set up hand signals with Captain Jimmy as the boat slowly followed the edge of the reef. We watched as his signals told Jimmy to go forward or stop. When he signaled to stop, the boat listed as we all pressed against the side to see what Colin was seeing. Colin studied the area and came aboard. He stood tall and smiled. "This looks like a good spot."

Colin described what he saw. "These types of formations are interesting to explore. The reef is split yet still connected on the north side. We can swim down and see what's at the bottom unless it's below 130 feet. Sometimes there's a tunnel we can swim through. If not, we'll swim to the outside, around, and back up shallow—depending on the current. Since this is new even to me, you need to follow me unless I signal otherwise. Everyone understand and agree?"

Without hesitation, we quickly geared up, jumped in, reassembled on the sandy bottom forty feet blow, and swam to the edge of the abyss.

The wall was sheer and dark. It plunged hundreds of feet. Puffy clouds covered the sky. No sunbeams were sent to pierce the depth.

A split in the reef formed a V-shaped canyon. Many millions of years ago there must have been a mammoth underwater upheaval that caused the reef to break away. It had sat there over the millennia, waiting until today to be discovered.

Colin counted divers and gave an "OK" sign before proceeding. I was the first behind him. I dove headfirst toward the corner of the V. The deeper I went, the darker it became. There were no sounds. I looked up for other divers who were silhouetted in the surface light and straddled by the sheer black face of the canyon walls. Colin and I hovered at ninety feet and waited for our eyes to adjust to the darkness. We saw an undercut ten feet below. I felt haunted by the quiet lure of its blackness. When we dropped to 110 feet, a glowing blue light blasted through a downward sloping passage, revealing a wide opening to the other side. It beckoned to us to explore it. Colin motioned me to swim through it and wait for the group.

I stopped abruptly as I came face-to-face with the largest lobster I had ever seen. My narcosis made the centurion two or three times larger than what it must really have been. As I swam over, it waved its long antennae and marched toward me. I was probably the first diver it had ever seen. It must have been wondering what I was.

I drifted into the passage and nervously swam deeper through the opening. Narcosis took a strong hold of me, challenging my ability to focus, and I grew concerned that when I emerged on the other side, I would exceed the 130-foot depth limits for recreational divers. Narcosis made me punchy. I began laughing at the wonder. I studied my surroundings, hoping I could recall what I was seeing. Between narcosis and dim light, it would be difficult to remember all this. I swam close to the ceiling to avoid wandering too deep.

I hovered and waited in the silent depth. Stems of black coral and the outlines of curling wire coral clung to the wall around the opening. Above me was the blue glow of the surface, and below was the blackness of deep water. One by one, others in the group emerged. Colin came through last and resumed the lead. The current strengthened from the north. We spiraled our way around and up the open-water side of the reef. On top, it was teeming with fish. Large schools of grunts and goatfish turned patches of the reef to a bright yellow underwater garden. They were tightly packed and more concerned about the current than they were about us. What bothers fish most about divers is the sound of our bubbles. That and our aggressive approach.

The growing current carried us swiftly back to the boat. We made a long safety stop at fifteen feet. All eyes peered on the canyon below for the three minutes we hung on the bar draped over the side of the boat. None of us would forget the journey into inner space where narcosis twisted our senses in that timeless, soundless, euphoric dark of the deep.

You can guess what the buzzing was all about back on the boat.

I felt privileged to be among the first humans to visit this place. Before this dive, I had assumed that with the age of this world and the vast number of people before me, there could exist no such place. But here in the deep was an inner frontier where I could lay my soul knowing no one had been there before.

We stood on the *San Sally*, talking about what to name the site. All new sites, after all, must be christened with a fitting name. Our brains searched for ideas. Creativity ran amok. Names were offered. Some dumb. Some very dumb. It was a canyon, a cut, a split reef, an abyss, a swim-thru, a grotto, and a pinnacle. Mostly, we described it as a canyon. Rich suggested using the name of the dive shop back in Connecticut that sponsored his group, Orbit's Marine.

Colin thought this place would make a good permanent dive spot. Although it was a long way from the resort, it would become one of the most sought-after sites on the island. Colin used an accurate art/science called dead reckoning to pinpoint its location. Mariners and navigators still practice it even though it has been largely replaced by Global Positioning System (GPS).

Boat captains and divemasters knew these waters well and could tell at a glance where they were. Whenever they dropped anchor, they were within a few feet of the dive site. In the 1980s, dive sites were not recorded. It was a way of protecting them from over-diving. Finding them came from skills acquired through local lore. Having been to most of them many times over the years, I defined my own landmarks in my dive logs and underwater maps. Technology, however, eventually ended all dive site secrecy.

***

Since we'd first discovered Orbit's Canyon in 1988, the island had been developed by an international corporation that introduced hundreds of divers weekly to the island's pristine and infrequently visited dive sites. Although the inn shared its knowledge and location of the dive sites, Orbit's Canyon was among the few they held back to preserve its untouched features. Locals told me the corporation sent a spy boat to follow the inn's dive boat, took a GPS reading, dropped a mooring, christened it with a name of their own, and began daily visits to the site with sixty divers. Like overfishing, they changed the underwater landscape and impacted the environment. To most, the truth of Orbit's Canyon will never be known. But as Paul Harvey, once the most listened-to radio voice in America, said at the end of his 1951–2009 program, "And now you know the rest of the story."

* * *

When the boat moored at "Avalanche," I had to surrender to the changed name, but nothing would rob me of what I knew. I dove in and glided down the familiar V-shaped canyon into the darkness below. I slipped under the deep ledge. That old mammoth lobster was long gone. A light shone from the other side, just like it had fifteen years before. In this world of instant change, it is gratifying to know some things never do.

When I got back on the boat, another diver approached. "You dove that like you've been here before. Have you?" I gazed over to the site and quietly replied, "Yeah, a few times."

* * *

Orbit's Canyon—Avalanche—call it what you want. They changed it to a name without meaning—to a past relabeled and a history erased.

I sit on the porches of changing times, and I see the older folks pushed "off the stage of life" by a younger, faster generation eager to change the landscape while ignoring the pioneers who carved the path on which they now walk. Their vision is blindness. But still, they drink beer to celebrate themselves. Perhaps, in my aging years, I have become protectively cynical.

Could I ever have been one of them? Whose story could I have trampled? Whose path could I have renamed? I was pulled back to my earlier days when I owned the world—to a time when I changed the landscape, embraced new values, and reinvented history by ignoring it.

* * *

I stood in the cockpit of a B-17, the Flying Fortress—the famous World War II bomber. It had machine-gun bubble windows all around like warts on a whale. I stood in a museum cutout version with a surround screen out the front window showing what the pilot saw. "Press the button and see what happened," so said the small sign. I heard screams of men and the cockpit chatter between the pilot and crew. Enemy aircraft buzzed around like angry bees. Bullets flew—sounding like nuts and bolts rattling in a tin pail. The crew yelled, "Bandits at nine o'clock!" I thought, *What a great model to help people experience and appreciate what their fathers did during that war.* I thought about the brave men who flew them and how many gave their lives so I could stand there free at that very moment.

I felt the presence of a slight old man standing next to me. I looked at him, nodded, gave him more space, and looked back at the model. He leaned forward and gently placed his hand on the captain's chair. "This was my seat."

"Excuse me?"

"This was my seat. I was the captain. I piloted eighteen missions in Europe in this plane."

"Oh." I turned my attention back to the model.

My sin was plain. I must have once been one of those cocky young kids who cast the likes of the now-me aside. Unwittingly, but so. If only I could go back and find that heroic pilot, I would look into his eyes and just say, "Thank you." But that opportunity is lost, and most likely the old warrior is now gone.

Years later I found myself standing before a mothballed Lockheed P-38 Lightning airplane on display at March Air Reserve in Moreno Valley, California. Two veterans sat with their legs crossed while they drank coffee, smoked cigarettes, and spoke softly to each other. I approached and asked them about the plane. They launched into stories of rocket raids and photo reconnaissance. When they were finished, I choked out, "Thank you." They nodded. "No, I mean thank you for making it possible for me to grow up in freedom."

When we come into this life, we are given only a small space in time. Our paths overlap with those behind or yet to come. We have neither the past nor the future. We are in constant collision with someone else's trail, and this is the great battlefield where our sense of purpose and worth get kicked in by the young and the fast.

Homes of old friends, sweethearts whose tender lips we kissed, and familiar faces all step aside for young people to write their own stories.

They change the landscape, just as we did long ago. We discover that our past is not their duty to keep.

Should we not visit, or do we get sent back to our yesterdays to be reminded of the shortness of time and the foolishness of squandering what little we have?

THOSE STUPID DEAD PLASTIC FISH

DIVE LOG

Date: January 2003
Location: Small Wall, Bonaire, Netherlands Antilles

The boat seemed to shake from the first-day dive jitters. The ride out was somber. This solemn mood would be temporary, especially when they discovered what I had in store for them. While on the same boat as me, no one was safe from my antics. No one.

They had waited months for this well-deserved trip. The night before, they had partied on the mainland and exchanged dive stories. "This time tomorrow we will be there," they chanted. Were they not the same ones I had seen at yesterday's dive orientation? What had become of the spirit so vivid and brilliant the previous night?

They sat as zombies. If they talked, they neither listened nor spoke coherently. They set their gear up backward. They wondered where they had stowed the mask that they held in their hands. Other belongings lay strewn across the deck. They wiggled and squirmed into their wet suits on the dock, knowing it would be thirty minutes before they dove in. Some engaged in quiet conversations, trying to find one good reason why they should postpone the first dive.

This was "get the jitters out" day. Any instructor can recognize the signs of diver stress. Most of the divers had not been down for at least a year, and it was doubtful that anyone had taken a pool refresher. Some had boarded with new gear still in the bags and boxes from the dive shop. I recall my own nervousness and silence on the ride out, which is how it was so easy to recognize it in others. I could sense the questions piling up in their minds. *Will I remember how to set up my gear? Will I freak out when I hit the water? How do I clear a flooded mask? Will I make a fool of myself?* Welcome to the club. Unless divers have been down within the last few months, no one escapes "jitters day." No one.

My compassion searched for a magic pill for the crippling stubborn nervousness I saw in divers that, sometimes, would not subside until the week was over. This was not a good way to make great memories.

If these were my students, what would I do? Time for introductions. I meandered around and sat next to the ones with dilated pupils staring off into space. "Hello. My name is Jeff. What's yours? How are you this fine morning? Isn't this a great day for diving? It's a little scary, this first dive. Oh, I'm sorry. I didn't mean you. Look around. Everyone's a little nervous. It's natural. First-day jitters, you know. No, you're not the only one. We all are. Hell, I've been diving for years, and I still get nervous on the first dive. So tell me, what makes you a little nervous? Ah, that happens to me, too. Here's what I do…"

It's amazing how far a little empathy will go.

I made a slew of new friends on the boat ride to the first dive. It's like being the door greeter in a store or at a conference. Everyone remembers the greeter.

* * *

My mind drifted back a few years to the pool sessions with my brand-new, shiny students. I found myself at pool's edge. Pondering, I looked into the deep end and tossed in a green net sack filled with PVC pipes and fittings. I watched it bubble as it sank. I was preparing for the "extra session." Students wandered to the edge, looking into the depth at the last remaining bubbles burping from the sack. "What's that?" they inquired.

"It's for a contest of sorts," I said, shrugging as I evaded additional explanation.

The required scuba pool sessions had already been completed. Students had performed all the exercises. They had studied, passed the tests, and signed off on the mound of legal paperwork. But there frequently remained a question about student readiness for the open water. Bronx, the master instructor, and I compared our assessments of individual comfort levels. When we announced that there would be an "extra" pool session, the students cheered, validating our premonitions.

The extra pool session was not to perform training exercises. Instead, we had come to play. Playing took their minds off the newness of the unnatural act of breathing air underwater. We sent students down to make a rectangular box from PVC pipes in the green net sack. By concentrating on the task, they did not focus on their anxiety.

The briefing was quick so as not to give them too much time to form strategies. The two teams looked intently at the net bag. It contained enough parts to make two rectangular boxes. The objective was to be the first team to present a completely assembled box of the proper size and shape.

At the signal, divers assaulted the net bag. Forty pieces of pipe were soon scattered across the bottom. A frenzy of bubbles churned the surface as teamwork came together by accident. According to the rules of engagement, they had to select pieces as needed from a community pile. We awarded extra points for creative cheating, sabotaging the efforts of the other side, and making new rules on the fly.

During the frenzy, my job was to maintain student safety and ensure one team did not get too far ahead of the other. Trickery topped the menu as I slid in to "help" the leading team. I raided the supply pile, conspicuously stashing stolen booty in my gear. Students, searching for the final piece, discovered it stuck in my gear and lunged to claim it. I gave nothing up without a good fight. I fled. They followed in pursuit. During the foray, opposing team members took advantage of the diversion, invaded the enemy camp, and dismantled their box. At times, the losing team, knowing they were hopelessly behind, abandoned the mission and launched an all-out attack on the other team.

We burned through air on those dives. Laughing under water drains air tanks quickly. They surfaced ready for open water.

* * *

I floated back to the present—back to Bonaire on this balmy January morning in 2003. *If only I could bring a net bag filled with PVC pipes on these trips.* Not practical. I had brought something smaller. And it loosened the stiffest of stiff divers and broke their hard-bound spell of nervousness. Creating distractions took their minds off their fear and helped prepare them for a good holiday. I loaded the pockets of my BC with "distractions" and set out in search of divers struggling with the jitters.

Divers watched me swim with fish close enough to be among them. Years before, Stephen Frink, a well-known photographer, taught me how to approach fish for up-close and personal experiences. After that, fish did not flee when I came near. Divers marveled and asked, "What's your secret? How do you do it?"

"Magic."

Such magic only made me more believable when I captured little creatures to give divers their own up close encounter with life under water. Imagine what I could do with pretend creatures!

* * *

Holly has got to be the most nervous diver I have ever met. Nervousness oozed out her pores, even under water. She hid behind pushy behavior and disinterest in anything anyone had to say. She was an avid uptight life hider. Looking good was her priority. Holly wanted the world to see her in a positive light, so she acted in a way to make others think she was someone she really wasn't. Pretending gets to be a full-time job, and after a while the only one being fooled was Holly. But she was not alone in the world. The world is full of Hollys.

Holly dressed flawlessly. Her personal grooming was immaculate. She permitted nothing to ever be out of place. Her nails shone with the shiniest of hard polish. Her hair didn't risk straying out of place. Her waterproof eye makeup and lipstick didn't dare run in the wettest of salty seas. Her dive gear was color coordinated—pink and pink. She had pink fins, pink gloves, pink mask, pink snorkel, pink weight belt, and pink splashes of color on her BC. She even brought her own pink weights.

Divers down. Where's Holly? Easy to spot. I looked for pink. There she was, only fifty feet away, looking impeccable as she kept her fearful distance from the reef by sculling with her hands as fins sat limp at the end of her legs. I prepared for the gig. I pulled the "distractions" from my pocket, selected the perfect prop, and swam to intercept Holly.

With cupped hands, I beckoned her to look. She looked at my hands and then at me. I motioned for her to take it. She refused with a contemptuous frown and backed away. I persisted. With an *Oh, very well* look, she rolled her eyes and reluctantly opened her hands, where I placed the creature without letting her see what it was. I closed her fingers around it, pressing to make sure she would feel it. I released my hands. We both watched with intent. Slowly she opened her fingers. Out floated a small yellow plastic fish with eyelashes and a smile. It bobbed and wobbled in the water. Holly was not amused. She turned her back on me and left the little creature abandoned in the sea and swam off.

I had failed but was not yet defeated.

I swam ahead of Holly and peered into a crevice. While she swam by, I caught her attention, motioned for her to come see my find. I pointed into the crevice. She looked into it, looked at me, and shrugged. I pointed again. Same response. I pulled her close to the crevice for one last chance to point out the creature within. She appeared annoyed and disinterested. In a last-ditch effort, I plunged my hand deep into the crevice and quickly withdrew it with a start. The creature had attached itself to my finger! Shaking my hand violently, I tried to throw off the impaling beast, but it held tight. It swallowed my entire index finger! It startled Holly, but she simply turned and swam away. I pulled the plastic shark from my finger and put it away.

Getting the best of Holly seemed hopeless. She was a hard case. I approached the dive boat and found her holding the down line while making her safety stop. One last attempt. I swam up to her with an orange fish on the inside of my mask. She looked at it, looked at me, and without expression headed for the surface.

Strike three. I was out!

Divers removed gear and set tanks up for the next dive while talking about what they had seen. Then came the blurting question from Holly, "Who was that with those stupid… dead… plastic… fish?" No one fingered the perpetrator. Uninterested in pursuing the matter further, she quickly dismissed it.

I always wondered how plastic fish could be either stupid or dead.

Holly was the ultimate challenge for my antics until Phil, whom you'll meet in the next chapter.

* * *

Carla was an underwater naturalist and fierce protector of the environment. On the arm of her wet suit was a badge with "Reef Cop" embroidered on it. When she saw offenders, she swept in to correct poor behavior and pointed to her badge. She took her mission seriously. I found a mound of sand created by burrowing clams. I discreetly placed Mr. Frog on the top of the mound and swam away. Because Carla was a naturalist and had never seen a creature like it, Mr. Frog caught her attention. Mr. Frog, after all, was a poisonous African tree frog and very far from home. When she was within a foot of it, I raced in, grabbed Mr. Frog and sent a cloud of sand into the sea, removed the regulator from my mouth, scarfed up the creature, pretended to chew and swallow my prey, and smiled at Carla, who watched in gaping horror. She pounded at my arm and growled through her regulator. Then I spit out the stupid, dead, plastic frog. Later I received a stern lecturing. Like I said, Carla took her reef cop role seriously.

Doesn't anyone have a sense of humor?

* * *

As divers swam the reef, they looked down, sideways, and backward, but seldom up. Suddenly, an orange octopus dropped in front of their masks. Reactions were memorable. If they tried to grab the octopus, I jerked it back on its string tether, which always elicited *I'll get even* looks. Even on the dive boats, anyone sitting near the dive platform became easy prey for the orange octopus being lowered from the upper deck.

* * *

Nothing was spared from my antics. Not even fish. I tormented a grouper. It sucked up my shark and swam away, its jaw moving from side to side. This was not an ordinary meal. The grouper spit out the shark and carried it sideways over the edge of the wall and dropped it—never to be seem by human eyes again.

* * *

Damsels are among the prettiest of sea fishes. Imagine a cute fish with eyelashes and lipstick. That's a damselfish. They are also the most aggressive and fearless of all sea creatures. Size means nothing to them. If they were any larger, diving would be unsafe. They are the most territorial of all. I wedged Mr. Frog in the crack of the coral reef, waiting for an unsuspecting passing diver. Ms. Damsel, not amused with this interloper in her neighborhood, repeatedly darted in and out of her hideaway, sizing up the intruder. She swam backward, slapping the frog with her tail. The frog took the beating. Power to the damsel. She dislodged it, carried it to the edge of her territory, and expelled it from her kingdom. Where's the camera during such a Kodak moment?

***

As divers caught on to my tricks, I had to resort to other deceptive antics. Fake doubloons, carefully hidden in the sand, were always big hits with new divers. This took a little planning and recruiting an accomplice. During the briefing, the divemaster told us to keep an eye out for them. One diver, upon discovering such a doubloon, took it back home to an assayer to have it appraised.

***

Turnabout is fair play. Kevin showed me a rubber great white shark that fit over his arm. He boasted that before the holiday was over, he would surprise me. On the last dive of the trip, I was spending a few peaceful moments on the safety line, saying goodbye to Planet Ocean. A shark appeared in the corner of my mask. I recoiled. Kevin swam away laughing.

***

Customs agents peered at the plastic creatures. They looked at me in disbelief and then back at them. Reactions varied, but I had never been held in customs for bringing home dead plastic fish. In my bag of surprises were sharks, octopuses, eels, turtles, frogs, yellow fish, orange fish, blue fish, seahorses, whales, sea lions, and crabs. For the next 738 dives, they were as essential a piece of gear as a snorkel, a mask, or a backup regulator.

I enjoyed my underwater games more with those from whom I could win a laugh or chuckle. I began to appreciate that quality and found myself more attracted to people with a sense of humor than those who took themselves too seriously. In retrospect, I turned the "humor-o-meter" on my closest friends and, not surprisingly, they all rated high in the humor department.

* * *

Casual divers seldom escape the nervousness awaiting them on the first day of diving, but their apprehension can shrink with the right amount of distraction. Those who dove with me knew what to expect, and that pushed my creative antics to the intellectual level. I learned to put surprise on my side. Divers may have learned what to expect, but they never knew when or where I would strike next. They could be anywhere, those stupid… dead… plastic fish.

REVENGE OF THE SEAHORSE

DIVE LOG

Date: August 2006
Location: Bloody Bay Wall, Little Cayman Island, BWI

I knew no one would believe me if I hovered over my rare find so early in the dive. Given my history of tricks, after all, I did have a credibility issue.

Adrianna described the dive site as a jigsaw puzzle of large coral heads in the sand bed twenty feet below. She told us to look for stingrays in the sand and seahorses at the edges of the coral heads. Seahorses!!?? They are a prized find. Let's go!

I donned equipment and rushed to be first off the boat. I jumped in and raced to search for seahorses. They were hard to find, but whoever spotted them earned bragging rights for a few minutes after a dive. I was in luck. I came upon a small, dark seahorse with its tail wrapped around the base of a sea fan. I waved for Ed's attention and showed him what I'd found. He moved in and then summoned the attention of other divers. One by one they filed in for a closer look and photos.

Phil swam in the near distance, unaware of the find. Ed got his attention, but when Phil saw me, he assumed it was just another Jeff trick and that what was there was really a plastic look-alike. Ed persisted. Phil agreed to take a look but remained suspicious for a dupe.

When he saw the seahorse, Phil was pleased, and he looked over to Ed and gave him an approving *OK* sign. He adjusted his camera and carefully maneuvered for a close-up. His strobe blasted light on the seahorse. Phil repositioned himself and took another, and another, and another.

I swam back in for another look. Phil looked at me with great satisfaction. I pointed to the seahorse. Phil smiled with his eyes. I moved closer and suddenly lunged for the seahorse, pulled it from its hold on the sea fan, shook it in the water, removed my regulator, and bit it in half. I spit out the head and held the tail high as I offered it to Phil.

Suddenly the sound of bubbles blurted loudly to the surface from the large number of witnesses. Masks quickly flooded as lines of laughter broke the mask seal. I sucked down air with my own laughing.

For years, Phil had been on to my tricks. It was impossible to lure him in. He was too quick to fall for my antics. This one had taken some doing and some coordination with divemaster Adrianna and Ed. Months earlier while in a San Diego gift shop, I had found the perfect "prop" in a jar of sun-dried seahorses. I bought two just in case one didn't make the journey to the Caymans.

I knew my days of trickery were ending. Divers who knew me were suspicious even when I pointed out a genuine living sea creature. Figuring that my seahorse caper with Phil could never be upstaged, I decided to retire as the underwater trickster.

The trip ended. It was time to go home. We had a three-hour layover in the Cayman airport. I wandered around in shops and discovered a small bag containing half a dozen plastic fishes. I couldn't resist. I paid for the package and carefully hid it in my backpack. Perhaps this sea creature charlatan had retired, but not the kid inside.

GOODBYE, *SAN SALLY*

TRAVEL JOURNAL

Date: July 2008
Location: Riding Rock Inn, San Salvador, Bahamas

I found her cowering in the corner—a child grown old and forgotten. No one had the heart to finish her off. She was already beat up when I first met her, but this is what becomes of all of us with the passage of time.

The Riding Rock Inn (RRI) showed up on my radar in 1988. The inn was a 1950s-style motel setting with its dining room, bar, and all twelve rooms a mere few feet from the water's edge. Rooms were small. Lacking amenities, they offered only a comfortable bed and a hot shower. But who cares? We came here to dive.

James Carter Williams, a prominent local businessman, purchased, restored, and reopened RRI in 1986. He offered work to anyone who wanted it and gave more back to the islanders than anyone before and since his time. Over the years he remembered my face but never the name. Upon my arrival, he always greeted me by firmly grasping my hands with both of his. He looked into my eyes and told me how good it was to see me again. Perhaps it was his hospitality that kept me coming back year after year. Sadly, he died from cancer in 2006. His children became my extended family.

San Salvador was a favorite for serious divers. A constant breeze helped keep the mosquitos at bay. The 150-foot water visibility with a sandy bottom gave the shoreline an azure glow—like the ones in the brochures. Some think those pictures are enhanced by airbrushing or Photoshop. They're not.

The sandy beach ran out to the edge of the wall that deepened until it hit reef's edge in forty to sixty feet of water. The deep-water side of the reef was home to some of the steepest and sheerest walls in the world. A national research foundation sent a robot down to check the depths out at eleven thousand feet in one place!

At reef's edge were cuts, holes, chimneys, tunnels, and sand shoots to provide varied passage to the outside wall. In some places, monster chunks of the reef had split away, making deep black canyons with interesting places for the advanced diver. The variation of entry points to the deep blue kept the sites unique.

Over the years, I made almost three hundred dives along the western and southern reef that surrounded this twelve-by-five-mile island. Now, on this 2008 visit, I was eager to settle in and spend my first day taking a stroll down the path to the marina and let memories take me back.

- In 1988 I sat with my nose smashed against the window of the plane. The clarity of the water and the shallowness of the sea made the entire region look like a blue marble cake. Swirls of shallow sand and deeper water wandered for miles. Tiny islands and secluded beaches dotted the landscape and sent my romantic imagination spinning out of control. I vowed I would sail from island to island and explore every inch of sand. I envisioned setting my anchor on the leeside, watching the sun set and the moon rise while sipping mint juleps with my topless damsel.

- During the first-night orientation, divers were given boat assignments. Mine was the *San Sally*. After hearing a little history about the dive boats, I raced to the marina to see what she looked like. She was a confiscated forty-foot wooden boat repurposed for diving after her life in the drug trade. The entire deck was canopied with a hard top where you could see all the layers of paint. Chunks of the boat had been chewed away from collisions with dock pilings. *So, I thought, this scow is going to be our dive boat for a week? They've got to be kidding.*

- We seldom went south because we had to endure *San Sally*'s forty-five-minute lumbering to get there. She leaked. She moaned. She creaked. She listed easily. No one cared about protecting the boat—it would be impossible to tell the difference between an old and a new dock wound. Over the years I was surprised she was still there, yet she became our "beloved dive boat." One day she vanished, replaced by newer boats, but I never found the affinity for them that I did with *San Sally*.

- It was a cloudless day with the water temperature a relaxing 84 degrees. Visibility easily exceeded 150 feet. I stepped off the back platform of the *San Sally* on my first dive. I settled in the sand and adjusted my gear. I found myself face-to-face with a two-foot Nassau grouper that came over to greet me. Its greenish body could change color instantly to match its surroundings. I reached over to say hello. Surprisingly it did not back away. The skin under its mouth was soft and supple. Its head was hard and the rest of its body coated with a slime to protect it from parasites. An experience like that was a good omen.

- *San Sally*'s engine died in deep blue water. While waiting for a tow, we dropped a line overboard and dove down, hoping to encounter a passing large creature, but all we saw was the surrounding and featureless cerulean blue. Without that line it would have been easy to lose orientation and control.

- I spent many a night mapping the moon as it set over the sea—measuring the width of moonbeams for another book that I haven't started yet.

- In 2003, I met an affable couple sitting alone at dinner. They were US expatriates living on the south side of the island. Hungry for new conversation, they invited me to join them. I told them of a long-ago adventure where a man gave me passage on his property to look down an Atlantic blowhole. While exploring it, I became curious about the man's efforts to build a self-sustaining property on the remote south end of the island. As fate would have it, I found myself sitting across the table from the same couple who had given me access to the blowhole fifteen years before.

- Over the twenty-three years between my first and last visit, children grew up and old men disappeared. New buildings appeared, old ones collapsed with age, and others were never finished. Bulldozers were left to rust and covered with clinging vines. Piles of dredged sand had never been moved and became homes for fully grown pine trees. Young girls married, made babies, and began new generations. The original fleet of dive boats, the *San Sally* and the *Sea Fan*, had long since vanished. *Sea Fan*'s name board found its new home in the Driftwood Bar. I wonder whatever became of *San Sally*.

* * *

I wandered around to the far side of the marina. My eye caught an old wreck of a boat with a familiar outline peering out from behind a larger craft. There was not much left of the paint. Broken pieces of wood were strewn across the deck, and algae grew thick on the bottom. She was old and no longer seaworthy. Even the dock lines looked frail.

I stood over her, gazing at her bow. Hiding in the corner, she had been placed there to die. She had been cast aside, too old and fragile to work and too much a part of the Williams family to become another wreck dive.

So there you are. Hello, my old friend San Sally. How are you? Long time no sea. Those who never knew what you were might see only a storyless, abandoned wreck, but I know differently. Are you the view of my future? How I fear that what I see in you will become me in my fading years. Tell me, old friend—allay my fears.

San Sally quietly rocked with the waves coming in and out of the marina. She creaked and bobbed and said nothing. How could she? She was just an old boat.

CONRAD

TRAVEL JOURNAL

Date: June 2013
Location: Peter Island, British Virgin Islands

We walked through the jungle to visit one of the most opulent places in the Caribbean. We passed through someone's front yard that was as well kept as the best of five-star palaces, yet it was a picture of the worst of poverty and best of someone's happiness.

I found a spunky lady working in the grocery store. Her job was cashier. She looked at my items and told me how to cook them and what to eat as a side dish. She acted like a person in charge. She was... It said so right on her name badge: "Patty, Person in Charge." One day she commented on a T-shirt I had picked up in the Cayman Islands. Asked if I was a diver. Said she was, too. Every time I went into that store, I searched for her. Can't say why. Well, it's not that I can't, but I don't know. As I waited in her line, another cashier attempted to pull me to her vacant checkout counter, but I refused. I had a need to flirt with this person in charge... this Patty person. One night, on the way home from work, I stopped for a loaf of bread and wine, and found myself face-to-face with talkative Patty. She flirted back. That frightened me and I ran, but I was intrigued by this mysterious woman and tracked her down before she left the store. Four years later we married.

I introduced Patty to sailing. She screamed when we heeled over. "There's no screaming in sailing," I said sternly. Except for what I taught her, she never took formal lessons. She became competent, and she quit screaming.

I signed up as crew on a boat delivery between the British Virgin Islands and the Chesapeake Bay. Patty begged to go as a galley slave so she could check "sailing the Atlantic" off her bucket list. The captain saw her sense of adventure and invited her along. The eight-day passage became a two-week test of nerves and stamina when most every system on the boat failed at one time or another, and failure came at the most inopportune time. I knew we were in serious trouble when the meteorologist on the satellite phone on the mainland said to the captain, "What the hell are you doing out there? Do you have any idea what's heading your way?" Before the ordeal ended, Patty was restricted to her bunk with broken ribs while she continuously yelled, "Oh shit! We're all gonna die. We're all gonna die." We were all so dehydrated, we passed the point of caring about living.

***

"Are you game for something a little tamer?" I timidly asked Patty.

"What do you have in mind?"

"I was thinking of renting a thirty-six-foot sailboat in the British Virgins for ten days. We can sail, get tanks and dive, or snorkel."

A month before the trip, we spent each weekend on our boat practicing the fine art of picking up mooring lines. On sailboats, the controls are in the back, making it difficult to see what's going on directly in front of the bow. We agreed Patty would take the helm and I would snag the mooring ball as we approached it. At first, we took several shots with a lot of yelling and cursing at each other. We advanced to using hand signals, and eventually Patty could bring the bow close enough to the mooring ball to gently kiss the boat without so much as an arm signal or "turn more, slow down." We packed our bags and headed to Tortola, BVI.

I'd better give you a little background. Being able to retrieve a mooring ball effectively is essential for two reasons: (1) In BVI, there are fewer mooring balls than boats vying for them. Missing a ball requires circling around for another chance that will not come because someone else will have already swooped in and snagged it. (2) Picking up a mooring ball requires coordination and communication. A lack of either can result in discarding all boat etiquette, mistreatment of one's beloved mate, name-calling, expletives, and unprofessional finger gestures between the helmsman and mooring-ball snagger—all to the delight of other boaters already settled in for afternoon entertainment. I didn't want us to be someone else's amusement.

* * *

Peter Island is quiet and blessed with an abundance of protective bays and coves. Our safe harbor of choice was on the north side and named Great Harbor. Because Peter Island was privately owned, there was a distinctive absence of bars. Drinkers flock to bars. No bars, no flocking, and no competition for mooring balls. With the ample supply of mooring balls, there was no opportunity to show off our skills.

Great Harbor became home for a week, and from there we day-sailed, snorkeled, dove. We had breathtaking adventures beating into the wind and Jimmy-Buffett-kind of four-hour return runs to our hidden cove with twenty-knot winds at our backs.

We learned that the Peter Island Resort was one bay over to the east. On our chart, we could see a narrow strip of land between our anchorage and the resort, and it would be safer to take our dinghy to bay's end and hike over.

We pulled the dinghy ashore and surveyed our surroundings. We found a winding path that vanished into a canopied jungle. At its entrance was a small structure that could have served a number of purposes and looked like a chicken coop on stilts without wire. It had dry palm fronds for a roof, and a few errant boards along the side for protection from the elements. There was also a pillow, the kind with a durable white canvas covering with blue stripes. It was propped up against one side, was dirty and aged, and looked as if someone spent a lot of time leaning against it while passing the time away "at the beach."

We zigzagged our way along the narrow path, ducking to avoid overhead branches, until we came to an opening of an encampment. On one side of the path was a garden with crops growing between the shale and limestone. On the other was a dilapidated concrete structure that was flaking away, exposing rusted rebar. There were two boarded windows with a door between them, also boarded up and held shut with a piece of rope. On the wall was painted "CONRAD," and it looked like graffiti applied by someone in a hurry. Next to the door was a rickety table almost completely covered with conch shells arranged in rows by size. Two signs, white paint on driftwood, were nailed to the front of the table. One said, "CONRADS CONCH SHELL SALES" and the other said, "10 + 20 DOLA." A money box sat nearby. If Conrad was away, a soul could buy shells on the honor system. His camp was orderly, oozing with poverty, and plush with a sense of serenity and personal contentment. His presence was pervasive, with everything well organized, leaves swept clean, and sun-bleached conch shells lining the path to help passers like us see the way. But something was missing... Conrad. We thought we would catch him on our return.

We continued our hike and soon came to the bay where we found the posh Peter Island Resort. We were met by a well-protected harbor with a well-made and well-appointed marina. Docking fees are normally posted, but not here. It was one of those "if you have to ask about our fees, then you probably can't afford to dock here" kind of marinas. I found the dockmaster and we talked fees. If a boater tied up dockside and became lost in the intoxication of Peter Island Resort opulence, he could be facing several hundred dollars for a few hours' stay—depending on the size of their boat.

Even though we were obvious interlopers, resort staff treated us with dignity as we wandered through a sprawling estate where the "cheap" rooms went for $1,200 per night during the off-season. The United States was still reeling from the recession of 2009, but there was no evidence of that at the Peter Island Resort. If you like romance, hammocks overlooking a vast expanse of water, long quiet beaches, five-star food, pampering, and exceptional service, this is the place to come.

We wandered down the path through the jungle to get to our dinghy. We encountered a local in Conrad's encampment tending to the garden.

"Hello, are you Conrad?"

"No, I'm just taking care of his place. Conrad was born in that shelter behind you. He lived his whole life right here and never left the island in all his days. He never went far from his shelter. He was the descendant of the slaves that were brought here centuries ago."

"You talk like he is gone. Where is he?"

"He is not here anymore. A few weeks ago they took him to hospice to die from a cancer."

We stood stunned and lost in an emotional stillness toward a person we had never met.

Other people passed by and asked the man about Conrad. They lamented his illness and told stories of their brief encounters with him.

I asked about the small structure down the path by the water.

"Conrad sat there in the shade waiting for people to come. He would greet them and invite them to look over his shells and to buy one. He treated everyone as God's children, and he was genuinely happy to see everyone. When he welcomed strangers, he wrapped both of his hands around theirs as he looked kindly into their eyes. With him, there was no hatred in this world. Everybody loved Conrad."

How ironic to see such social extremes touching one another and giving evidence that it was Conrad who was the one most at peace by having nothing. Conrad is gone now. He closed his eyes and left his legacy written on the shack, the same one where he was born.

SUCKED DOWN

DIVE LOG

Date: August 2014
Location: Cozumel, Mexico

We were out of control and spinning around in circles in the middle of sea garbage.

The dive briefing was simple. "For those of you who keep dive logs and want the name of a particular site, we do drift dives and will pass two or three dive sites in a single dive. Just write down whatever name you like. But remember this… You're on boat eighteen. Jump in and go with the flow until you run low on time or air. When you surface, inflate your safety sausage and wait for a boat to come to you. Don't attempt to swim to it. Questions? Great. Have a good dive." We would be zipping along at three to four knots. How could we just flag down a boat?

    I stood at the gateway to the sea at the side of our dive boat, looking down at the water. I spit in the water to measure the speed of the current. My spit didn't move. Where's the current? These waters were famous for them. Our boat bobbed in still water. How disappointing. I had come to experience lightning-rod current. Must be slack tide. We jumped in and got our bearings. Looked to the bottom. Rocks and sea mounds and sandy hills raced past us—or was it us racing past the bottom? Since we and the boat were drifting along at a high speed and the boat was our only reference, it appeared we were floating in still water. As soon as we descended, we were swept away by the current.

For the next forty minutes, I "yahoo'd" my way over the hills and valleys as I learned the ways of swift water diving.

Visibility was easily two hundred feet, and getting out of sight of other divers was not going to be a problem. Because it was our first time in these waters, we attempted to remain close to the divemaster. I didn't like the idea of floating around on the surface at dive's end, waiting to be spotted by the dive boat.

After two days, I discovered that by positioning my body in the current, I could slow down and have some control, or I could make myself fly as fast as the current. This became a handy method to ensure I remained close to Patty.

On our third day, we were the last divers in. By the time we descended, we were far behind the group. No problem—they were all still in view. Suddenly we were among them, and the divemaster gave us the signal to turn around. Nature can be a strange thing. The forceful current going south abruptly stopped and immediately whipped up to three knots going the other way. We returned in a slightly different direction and passed tall sand mounds with huge protruding boulders. Many of them had tunnels large enough to swim through. Schools of fish took refuge in them to rest and escape the current. They were alluring. How I wanted to explore them, but that would go against our decision to remain close to the divemaster.

I turned to check on Patty and flattened my body to slow down. I noticed a thermocline band of current sweep past me. A thermocline is a steep temperature gradient in water where temperature differences can be five degrees separated by inches. Usually, warmer water sits horizontally on top of cooler water. Thermoclines are easy to spot. They look like cellophane, making everything on the other side of it look wavy. I had been in them many times, but this one was markedly different in that it was vertical, not horizontal. And when I stuck my hand into it, the water was noticeably warmer and ran much faster than the current we were in. When Patty caught up with me, we got pulled into a fast lane of current that felt like tepid bathwater.

Our divemaster hovered at fifteen feet for his safety stop. We maneuvered near him and followed suit. Our three-minute mark came, and we began ascending behind the divemaster. I felt pressure on my ears. Instead of going up, we were descending. I yanked on Patty, thinking she wasn't paying attention, and she responded with a stern glare. I checked my depth. Twenty feet. I looked to the surface to find the divemaster being pulled in circles by a surface current. I kicked up, but to no avail. Twenty-five feet. I saw what looked like a tornado, and it felt like we were being pulled toward it. Thirty feet. I pumped air into my BC and kicked hard as I tried to push Patty toward the surface. Then I figured out what was happening. We were caught in a whirlpool with a downdraft current. They call these frightening events vortexes, and they occur when two opposing currents collide. I abandoned our attempts at swimming up and against the current and pushed Patty through the swirling bubbles, and that ended our descent. We had to repeat our safety stop. We continued to swirl around, but at least we weren't being sucked down.

After three minutes, we ascended to the surface only to find ourselves still in the struggle against the vortex. It had settled down to whirlpool stage, but it remained a powerful force. I looked around. Dozens of other divers were caught in it, as were boats, sargassum weed, plastic bottles, and other sea garbage. We were caught in the center of it, and the force of the whirlpool pushed all of us together along with boats and anything else floating about. Captains were unable to control their boats. They bumped into one another as the swirling current pulled us tighter and closer together against the disabled boats.

Crew from the boats feverishly pulled divers out of the water, and we huddled on deck, catching our breath and reeling from the horrific event.

"What's your boat?" asked a crewman.

"Huh?" I responded.

"Your boat. What's your boat number?"

"I don't know."

"Which resort are you staying at?"

"Scuba Club Cozumel."

"Didn't they tell you which boat number you were on?"

"Oh. Yeah. That. We're on boat eighteen."

For the next half hour, dive boats from various resorts shuttled divers to the proper boats. Only a few of us from our dive boat had gotten caught up in the whirlpool.

"How'd you like *that* ride?" said our divemaster with a broad grin.

"Does this kind of thing happen much?"

"All the time. I watched you playing with the thermocline and could see that you were about to get caught in the forming whirlpool. That was an unusually big one. They seldom go deeper than fifteen or twenty feet. Lucky you didn't get in the center. It's very disorienting. You did the right thing to swim away from it. How'd you know to do that?"

"I used to spend time in the dive shop back home listening as the old-timers traded stories. Boris, the dive shop owner, told of being sucked down in a whirlpool, and his buddy reached through it and pulled him out."

Being caught in a strong current can be intimidating to a diver unfamiliar with it. For that matter, anything new can be daunting. Here on Planet Earth we can escape fear by jumping away. Down below, the unknown can bring on an overpowering urge to get to the surface in a hurry. Long ago, one of my students asked what I feared the most as a diver. I said, "Panic, because it causes us to abandon all training, all reason, and it sends us into action that will do us the most harm."

You would think that after 1,231 dives, few things could frighten me. This dive reminded me that I must never forget that panic will always be a threat.

IRMA!

TRAVEL JOURNAL

Date: September 2017
Location: Grand Turk, Turks and Caicos

I tracked a tropical storm traveling too slowly for my liking. Those are the kind that can grow into terribly powerful hurricanes. She remained on a steady easterly path with not so much as a degree of turn to the north. The National Oceanic and Atmospheric Administration (NOAA), the most reliable source for storm tracking, had her on a trajectory to pass well south of us. By the time we arrived on the island, that slow-moving tropical storm had become a full-fledged hurricane named Irma.

Patty and I plan our Caribbean trips well in advance. We schedule them for August or September, when the water is the warmest and the fewest people are there. Yes, that's well into hurricane season.

When preparing for this vacation, I checked the National Hurricane Center website daily. I kept an eye on a southerly tropical storm with a medium probability of becoming a major weather event. NOAA storm models are reliable, and they projected that this storm would remain on a straight line well to the south of Grand Turk. It was bothersome since it was moving slowly over 85-degree water—a recipe for a powerful and dangerous storm. Although I had confidence in the National Hurricane Center predictions, I contacted islanders whose eyes were following the disturbance. They assured me it was an inconvenience that would bring heavy rain for a day, and high seas. While our plane was headed to Florida, the storm was upgraded to a hurricane.

In Miami, our airline carrier posted destinations where services had been canceled. Ours was not on the list. We boarded and flew to Providenciales (Provo) in the Turks and Caicos. When the wheels touched the ground, my phone buzzed: "A travel advisory is in effect for the Turks and Caicos Islands. If you are ticketed to this destination, you may cancel and rebook without additional charges or administrative fees." The message had been sent immediately after our plane had pulled away from the tarmac in Miami, when it was too late to act.

In Provo, we got in line to catch a plane returning to the United States. No seats. Forget the wait list—already dozens of names ahead of us. We decided if the storm hit, we'd be better off on Grand Turk.

After thirty minutes in a nine-passenger plane, Grand Turk came into view. There were no boats along the coastline. Not a good sign.

Irma defied NOAA predictions and turned to a northwesterly trajectory. She was no longer a passing annoyance. Irma had already pummeled the Lesser Antilles and gotten the attention of the authorities in the States.

We picked up our yellow golf cart—transportation for the next thirty days. The resort welcomed us back to our eleventh visit. We unpacked and drove around, visiting friends. Our first stop was at the dive shop.

"When did you move the boats to North Creek?" I asked.

"We did that just this morning."

"What's the word on the storm? I heard it was heading south of us."

"We had to get the boats into North Creek in case the storm changed its course and rough seas made it impossible to navigate into the creek. It's just precautionary. Sorry, but there won't be any diving until we know where that storm is going."

All we could do was wait and enjoy the beautiful weather and calm warm water. We were glad to be home. And we hoped nothing would come from all the storm preparation.

***

9/6 Wednesday

Irma was upgraded to a Category 4 storm and changed its direction—now it was heading directly toward us. We learned later that the American Embassy sent word for US visitors to leave and sent a plane to take them to Jamaica, since US airlines had canceled all flights to and from Provo.

The resort staff turned their full attention to storm preparation. They took in tables, chairs, and plants, and the art on the patio walls. Workers unpeeled the canvas restaurant cover from its frame and stowed it. Then they were sent home to tend to their families.

The resort closed. We were told that if the storm hit, we would have to leave. Leave? And go where? There was a storm shelter, they said. We would have to bring our own bedding, food, and water. Resort management was concerned about storm surge that could undermine the waterfront buildings. I convinced them that storm surge would be minimal because of its direction and the small size of the island. I signed a waiver and they allowed us to stay. They wanted us to move to the nearby Atrium, across the street and away from potential storm surge. I was apprehensive about the ability of the Atrium's wood structure to withstand the full brunt of the oncoming storm. I pleaded my case to remain in the main hotel, which had been built like a fortress. We were allowed to stay where we were. We were going to be the only ones at the resort until a cell tower technician moved into an adjacent room and the resort's food manager took the room directly below us. Even with surrounding company, we felt a sense of aloneness and doubt: Were we doing the right thing by staying where we were?

We stocked up on water, bread, peanut butter, crackers, candles, and extra batteries. We placed all our essential papers and anything needed for survival in ziplock baggies and stuffed them into our "ditch bag"—my backpack—and kept it within arm's reach. We filled wastebaskets with water and kept them in the bathtub for bathing and flushing the toilet. Before they left, hotel staff brought us kerosene lanterns, a microwave oven, and a toaster.

Locals crouched around sandbags, filling them by hand and with shovels, but few had any way to transport them to their homes. Our yellow cart became a sandbag shuttle.

The night was calm. We sat on the beach formulating contingencies with "what if" scenarios. One thing we had yet to appreciate was wind speed. A Category 4 storm produces sustained wind speeds beginning at 130 mph, and humans lose footing at winds greater than 70 mph. There would be no moving around once the storm hit. I hoped we had chosen wisely by staying at the resort.

We received frantic texts from my sister Sara after she heard we were in front of what meteorologists labeled a "nuclear storm" that would completely destroy anything in its path.

Patty lost email communication with her family. She looked at me and began crying. "What have we done? Are we going to be OK?"

"It's gonna get hairy, but we're in the strongest building on the island."

I held her until it was time to turn in.

9/7 Thursday

Quietness blanketed the morning. The air was still, and there was little activity around the island. Ominous dark clouds appeared in the east and quickly overtook the sky. Overnight, Irma had been upgraded to a Category 5 storm with a projected heading of fifty miles south of our island. The wind speed could exceed 160 mph. We drove around one last time, offering to help fill and schlep sandbags. We found an open store and picked up more water. The roads were abandoned. Islanders hunkered down. Animals took to their natural hiding places. Frigate birds, however, relished the increasing winds by soaring in circles high above.

I encountered a quivering dog, shaking with its head lowered and its tail between its legs. It cowered and ran from me when I approached. I told another person who knew the owner of the missing animal. She made a phone call, and the dog and its owner were soon reunited. I tried imagining the consternation if they could not find the animal before the storm hit.

I stood at the hotel entrance watching utility poles sway like palms and the eastern sky become ominously blacker by the moment. The speed at which weather conditions deteriorated gave me a heightened appreciation of the power of Mother Nature. If I had been in denial about a dangerous storm, what I was witnessing ended the fantasy that we were out of harm's way. Short bursts of deluges came with warm water that felt more like rain blobs than drops. When the deluge became a constant downpour, the wind increased, tearing leaves off the trees and sending the rain sideways, making millions of piercing knives. It was hard to believe that only a few hours earlier there was a dead calm. Irma had arrived.

Reports said the storm would max out at 11:30 p.m. We had a long way to go, and a lot could happen. The palm in front of our balcony became a wind barometer.

Pieces of ripped-apart corrugated roofing soared toward the sea like kites, becoming nature's most lethal weapon. I have seen movies with the heroes leaning forward, holding their arms up to protect their faces, and still able to move against hurricane-force winds with everything imaginable blowing by. What we were experiencing was living proof that Hollywood seldom represents reality.

We watched weather reports coming from the United States. Florida was frantically bracing for the storm. "Leave or die," authorities warned, but the state's gasoline supplies had been depleted, and all roads to safety became hopelessly clogged hundred-mile-long parking lots. Airports closed. No taxis. No way out. Many returned to their homes to crouch down and cling to one another.

1:46 p.m.—The television snapped and went blank, ending the minute-by-minute updates. The air conditioner went silent. Our room quickly heated up and became stiflingly humid. With power gone, the room became eerily quiet, reminding us that we had just been severed from the world. I could still text. "Leave or die" echoed through my head. We had no place to run. We were pinned in by 80 mph winds that were still 100 mph below what was coming. Our palm wind barometer still had its fronds as they clung "by their fingernails" to the main stem.

Each gust ushered in an increase in steady wind speed and shook the building and our confidence that we were safe.

3:00 p.m.—I had been exchanging texts with Richard, a friend and builder, who was about to put his new hurricane-proof building to the test. The connection distracted us from the threat outside. I hammered out one-word messages to my daughters and my sister Sara. Suddenly, there was a boom and our building shook. The cell tower on the ridge of the island failed, and lost was our last communication outlet. A sense of aloneness took us to a new depth.

3:30 p.m.—The entire top of the palm barometer—including all fronds and coconuts—snapped off and flew into the sea. I was astonished to see how far the wind could carry it. I thought about locals living in their shanties and what the US meteorologists had said about this being a "nuclear storm." The worst was yet to come, and already our building was shaking.

4:30 p.m.—Something huge hit the roof right above us with a deafening crash. I clutched our "ditch bag" and sat on the bed with Patty. For the first time, I sensed we were in real danger. I trusted the block walls, but we could be assaulted from the roof. I estimated wind speed in excess of 150. Everything rattled with a roar—the door, the windows, the building.

5:20 p.m.—Out the balcony door I could barely see the waterline through the sheets of rain. There were no waves and it looked like very low tide—pushed away by the wind. With our building this strong and feeling what it was doing to a concrete and block structure, my thoughts constantly went back to the locals in their shanties.

Wind whistled and rain spurted through the doorstops and began flooding the room. I cautiously approached and put my ear to the door. The relentless pelting of rain sounded like loud radio static. I crammed towels along the threshold, but it was folly. Water flowing through the doorjamb reminded me of a scene in the movie *Titanic*, where the pressure from the sinking ship blew out the doors and flushed people to their death. The door to our room faced the hurricane. It opened to a landing and an enclosed stairwell that offered marginal wind protection. The door was held shut by a one-inch deadbolt. If that gave, things would instantly become very ugly and deadly. The wind would ravage our room and, depending on where we were, could whisk us out the balcony door. We were excruciatingly vulnerable.

7:30 p.m.—The wind speed reached 180 mph. I lost confidence in the integrity of our structure even though we were inside a fortress. It shook. It rumbled. I was convinced our door would be blown in or the roof would be ripped or peeled away, and we would be sucked out. We huddled in a corner in the most protected part of the room. For two hours we occupied ourselves with a game of twenty questions as darkness fell. We jumped whenever there was another crash.

With each surge of wind came a painful increase in pressure on my ears, followed by more intense shaking. I thought, *It's going to be a long night.*

The wind was trying to pry the building apart. The rain was horrific. How could anything outside survive? How were the islanders holding up?

8:15 p.m.—The center of the storm passed. Or were we in its eye? Would the fury of the storm shift to the west? If it did, we would have little protection. My mouth was cotton-dry with concern for our safety and the deadly unknowns that lurked outside.

9:00 p.m.—The winds dropped to a mere 60 mph. I opened the balcony door and stepped outside. Without lights it was impossible to see the extent of damage, but it was plain most of the trees were down.

9:30 p.m.—We felt it was safe to approach the door but were still fearful about opening it. The towels along the threshold were soaked, and I used them to wipe the sweat from my face. Exhausted, we passed out with a sense of relief.

9/8 Friday

Last night's rain had bloated the wood and kept the door firmly wedged in the jamb. Perhaps that was why it didn't blow in. I yanked on the doorknob and got concerned that it would break off and we would be trapped until someone might think to check on us. The doorknob held, but the door split. Didn't matter… It had already become collateral damage from the force of the rain.

I stepped into the landing area. It smelled like freshly cut greenery. Every nook, cranny, piece of wood, step, and railing was solidly covered with foliage ground by the wind into small pieces of sticky green confetti.

All the trees had been either blown over or denuded. None of the power poles had been spared. They had snapped or were pushed to a forty-five-degree angle. Electrical lines and smashed transformers littered the roads. Pathways and the road were impassable. But the sky was clear, the sun shone, and the storm had passed.

I walked up the street, stepping over and under branches. Coming my way was Joan, an islander who had spent the night alone with her dogs. We hugged and checked each other for injuries.

Most of the framed houses were destroyed from collapsed roofs, blown-in walls, or rain damage. Fallen trees and power poles isolated the entire area. It was not a matter of throwing a few "plan B" switches to restore the grid… The grid was gone. Islanders were cut off from the world. There would be no water, no sewer, no medical facilities, no communication. Food would spoil. Disease would spread. A simple abrasion could become a worrisome infection.

What was worse than the storm was the aftermath. Islanders wandered in shock amongst the rubble that had been their home. Some stood with their hands on their hips looking around, wondering where to begin.

In a nearby home, a rope line had been pulled between two trees and a woman had already begun cleaning out clothing. The walls of the house were still standing, but the roof was gone. This became a common sight throughout the island.

At the edge of the road was one of the wild island horses. It stood looking at me and made no effort to move. I approached slowly and spoke softly. A trail of dried blood ran down its head, between its eyes, and around its nostrils. When I was within a foot of its face, I put the back of my hand near its nose and on its mouth. I stroked the horse and examined the gash in its head. The animal was more in shock than injured. My mind began to wander. *Where do they go? How do they emerge safely?*

I walked past another blown-down house. On top of the pile of intertwined splinters, broken furniture, bashed-in appliances, and sand-filled shreds of clothing sat a small brown stuffed animal, unharmed by the storm.

Street signs had blown away or become twisted storm-torn remnants. A wooden stake impaled a tree as though someone with great power had thrown it like a javelin. The more I looked, the more scenes like this I saw.

Rumors quickly spread about prison riots and two convicted murderers who had escaped. There was talk of widespread looting, and people were warned to keep an eye out for the dangerous escapees.

The government declared a "state of emergency," which gave them powers unavailable to them during "normal times." Curfew was set for 7:00 p.m. Still, looters roamed and rummaged, hiding behind darkness. The police, in their exhaustion, became ineffective.

9/9 Saturday

I came across a man with his arm stuck between two pieces of a wall and jumped over the rubble to help. He was not trapped as it appeared but was feeling around for a broom originally stored on the other side of the downed wall. While helping him retrieve it, I heard a local calling my name.

"You must go back to the hotel. Someone from the government is looking for you."

The US Embassy had discovered there were two unaccounted-for US visitors and had found us way out on Grand Turk. They had commissioned a local government official to find us.

"The US Embassy got word of a prison escape, looting, and even murders," the official said. "It's too dangerous for you to stay here. You two are the only US visitors on this island. We are giving you one chance and one chance only to get off the island by way of a military transport if you elect to leave."

"I thought the airport was closed."

"Only for private and commercial carriers. We need to know your decision within an hour. This will give you time to pack your belongings and get to the airport. The military transport will take you to Provo."

"An hour to pack our belongings and somehow get to the airport without transportation and blocked roads?"

"You'll have to pack light and leave things behind. What is your decision?"

"What happens when we get to Provo?"

"In Provo you can contact the American Embassy and stay until the country reopens. When you get there, you'll be on your own, but away from all the troubles here."

Was the threat of lawlessness and escaped prisoners really as great as the official said? Locals didn't seem to be as concerned. Who better to talk to about the prisoner situation than a local? I came across a woman sitting outside her half-demolished house. Certainly, I thought, she would know. "Only two of them got out, and they both are back there now," she said. "One of the boys went to see if his mama was OK, and she tell him to go back where he belong. The other fella went home to see if his wife and baby were OK and then he walked back. Nobody had to go get them."

I talked to the local police. "They want to take you to Provo?" an officer said. "Are they nuts? It's worse than here. They have no power and no phones, and the airport is closed to commercial traffic—just like here. You won't find any taxi service. All the hotels are shut down. There's widespread looting. You'll get dropped off at the airport, and then you'll be sitting ducks with your luggage—no place to go, and no protection. The US Embassy in Provo is closed and the nearest one is in the Bahamas, and they're closed, too. You're better off staying right here."

We gave our response to the US representative. "You realize that by staying here, there is no known date when you'll be able to leave," she said. "But if that's your decision, so be it. Please sign these papers releasing the US government from any liability. And please leave us contact numbers for your next of kin. We will attempt to contact them."

We signed the papers, and the official left. We stood feeling a cloak of isolation and aloneness. We did not know when we would be able to leave or how we could get word back to family that we were all right. We had enough food and water for four or five more days. Then what? We thought about what we were giving up by remaining on Grand Turk and decided we had made the best decision.

9/10 Sunday

Thanks to the restoration of the hotel's generator, we had power and water. We "reported" to hotel management for cleanup duty. I was given a can of WD-40 and a basket of room keys. "None of the locks work," I was told. "They are clogged with sand. Flush them out."

I will never understand how tiny grits of sand can get jammed so deeply in the internal workings of locks—on both the front and back doors of the room and even on doors that were out of harm's way.

Within a day all the locks in the main part of the hotel were working. They sent us across the road to the Atrium, where a dozen more sand-filled locks awaited us. Hotel management was preparing to open the building to house outside help coming to restore island life. The Atrium was where they had thought we would be safer than in our hotel room during the storm. Half the Atrium's second floor was reduced to splinters. We would not have survived.

The kitchen at the hotel reopened for takeout food. Workers

reinstalled the canvas awning over the restaurant. The bar reopened. There was a flicker of new life. It was a positive sign that life would eventually return to normalcy.

9/11 Monday

A United Nations (UN) team of seven arrived. They stayed at our hotel and quickly befriended us. Jakob, the group leader, was a farmer from the Netherlands, and Geronimo, second in command, was a sheep farmer from Venezuela. The remaining five—four women and one man—were all Canadian.

9/12 Tuesday

We received word that a hurricane right behind Irma had turned north and dissipated. One less concern.

9/13 Wednesday

The UN team wasted little time in assessing the situation and delivered a sobering report to the government. Things were much worse than anyone thought—no sanitation, no water, no access to medical facilities, total loss of the power grid. Infection would spread rapidly. Looters roamed unchecked under the cover of dark. Local police were exhausted. Their report got the government's attention. They asked the UN to coordinate the restoration effort, and control began replacing the chaos.

A doctor from the closed hospital saw me climbing among piles of debris helping people and warned me to be careful; a cut could become infected, and there would be no medical facilities to tend to me.

The utility company cleared the roads of loose power lines, utility poles, and trees. We drove around looking to give help and found entire neighborhoods still under water that wouldn't or couldn't leach into the ground. Children made a game of jumping on half-submerged boxes while the adults attempted to cope with water flooding their homes almost a week after the storm. We watched men repair their roofs with corrugated tin that had blown off someone else's house. With roof intact, they relaxed with a sense of comfort.

9/14 Thursday

A relief team of police arrived from Provo and swiftly ended the widespread looting, but not before our hotel's generator fuel supply had been raided and visibly crushed the spirit of hotel management. The hotel's fuel supplies were reduced to a few days' worth with no known replenishments. How could the hotel provide quarters for all the help brought in to restore the island? Miraculously, the owner found a fuel source. A night security officer was hired to roam the perimeter.

Our golf cart became part of the recovery effort. I ferried the UN personnel around the island as needed. After the resort's fuel supply had been raided, I began checking the golf cart daily. Janet, the resort manager, came to me as I checked my own dwindling supply of fuel and examined a slow leak in the tire. "My husband owns a gas station," she said. "Take your cart to him to fix the tire and gas up. He's there. Go refuel now." His people pulled a nail out of the tire and refused to accept money, reasoning that the "yellow golf cart" was part of the humanitarian effort to help the islanders.

9/15 Friday

After we'd been here more than a week and severed from outside communication, the cell tower technician lent us his satellite phone. "It's against company policy to use this phone for anything but official business," he said, "but contact your families and keep it short. All you have is texting."

We found an open place where we knew satellite reception would be good, but our texts got lost somewhere. I frantically reentered phone numbers and resorted to short texts: "We're OK." When I was close to giving up, a text reply came from sister Sara. I choked with emotion when I saw her words.

As we were returning to our room, I stopped, dazed by the sight of new growth on a ripped-to-shreds tree. The more I looked around, the more growth I saw. Mother Nature can rebuild as quickly as she can tear down.

9/16 Saturday

The perimeter fencing around the airport had been completely restored. No threat of wandering animals on the runway when planes arrived. The airport reopened even though commercial service remained unavailable. We got word of a transport plane arriving with fifty UK military men, redeployed from a tour of duty in the Middle East. Their task was to rebuild the power grid. We joined hundreds of others in cheering as fifty soldiers deplaned. Estimated time to restore service—three to four months. They did it in three.

9/17 Sunday

Jakob, the lead UN person, took me aside. "When were you originally planning to leave Turks and Caicos?"
"October third is when we are supposed to leave."
"I'm giving you a heads-up on some inside information. You must not tell anyone. No one! It will cause a terrible panic. I just got word that Hurricane Maria turned and is now heading for Grand Turk as a Category 5 storm. All our efforts at restoration will be undone and will create island havoc. I've seen this before in other parts of the world. News of another storm like Irma could set the island on fire with panic. The airport will open to commercial traffic on Tuesday, and I'm advising you as a UN official and friend to make sure you'll be on a plane. Please take me seriously. I know these islanders are part of your family, and you've done more than enough to help. You need to get out while you can. If you don't, you'll be in grave danger and may not be able to get off for another month."

9/18 Monday

Word had already spread about approaching Hurricane Maria. The inside of the airport was closed and being used to house the UK militia. All flight information was conducted on the hoods of cars. We got a ticket and were told to be at the airport by 8:30 a.m. the next day.

9/19 Tuesday

"What time is your plane?" asked Janet from the hotel.
"Not until nine thirty. They told us to be there by eight thirty."
Janet looked at her watch. "It's seven fifteen. Quickly, finish your breakfast. You must go now. If you wait any longer, you may not get off."
Word of Maria had gotten out. Tension swept through the airport. Respect for waiting one's turn in line had been discarded. I found myself constantly squeezed away from being "next in line."
I elbowed my way back in, vowing to myself that I would not allow anyone else to take my turn. I gave my name to the man poring over manifest lists while he used the hot hood of the truck for a desk. "Your name's not here. You're not on any flights." He checked again. "Nope. Not here. Sorry."
I pointed to a heavyset man acting as a gate monitor. "That man over there… he put my name on the list yesterday."
The agent went to the man by the gate. They looked over at me. When he returned, he said, "You're on the wrong hood. You need to go over there."
I had to resume my disrespectful elbowing to ensure we didn't lose our seat on the right plane.
"Good thing you showed up when you did," said the agent for the right plane. "I was about to give your seats away." Thank God for Janet.
In Provo, we raced to the US carrier. They said the plane was almost full and we could get on but not sit together. After we left, only one other plane took off, a day later, before the Provo airport closed again.

***

We arrived home in the very early hours of morning. We awoke to trees with leaves, straight power poles, and American prosperity that was oblivious to the events in the islands. Culture shock. I kept a close watch on Maria. She had been downgraded to a Category 4 storm and was heading north and west of Grand Turk. On September 21, less than two weeks after Irma, Maria turned and slammed Grand Turk.

"What was it like, that hurricane?" we were asked. Hearing all that noise, listening to the high-pressure blast of paint-stripping rain, watching large chunks of buildings fly by, and hearing heavy things fall on our roof was nothing compared with the aftermath when we saw the emotional impact on these brave islanders who had no place to go. I witnessed their fear, their fortitude, their strength, their courage to find the blessings in life, and their will to survive. After the storm, they emerged from their homes and immediately set out to collect what they could and rebuild what they had lost. None of them complained or took pity on themselves. When asked how they fared, their responses were almost all the same: "We are all well—we are blessed."

Months later, I learned that the wind had gusted to an incomprehensible 220 mph on the ridge by the cell tower. We had, indeed, survived a "nuclear storm."

Perhaps it was best that we left when we could, but that did not lessen my sense of having deserted our friends on Grand Turk. We came close to feeling and experiencing what the islanders felt, but always in the back of our minds we knew that eventually we would be able to leave. For that reason, it was impossible to appreciate what the islanders live in day after day, year after year. They know they must rely on one another. They know their shelter will be damaged or destroyed again, and again, and again. But they get up the next day and rebuild. They live with the knowledge that there's always another devastating storm. This time, however, not a single person died from Irma or Maria. From what we witnessed, it was not a blessing, but a miracle.

I ponder the messages that come through experiences. I don't believe in accidents and wonder how what happened yesterday will guide my perspectives about today or tomorrow. Pictures and words don't tell the story. We are glad for having been placed in harm's way and grateful for the gift it gave us.

HEART ATTACK AT 50 FEET

TRAVEL JOURNAL

Date: August 18, 2018
Location: English Point—Grand Turk, Turks and Caicos

Didn't enjoy that dive. Can't say why. I've always liked this site. Could not seem to get comfortable. Stiffness in my neck sent muscle aches down both arms. Tried to shake it off. Got out of breath getting back on boat. I've been diving too much without a break. I need a day off.

Patty and I had just finished a romantic dinner at the Turks Head Inn. When we climbed back into our golf cart, I went into a rage.

"What's wrong?" said Patty.

"My cold cup has been stolen. It was right here when we went in, and now it's gone." I walked around, spewing sailor talk like a pro. I worked myself into a tizzy, to the point where breathing became difficult.

"It's just a cup," Patty said. "You never get worked up, especially with something as trivial as this. What's going on?"

I blamed my loss of control on being tired, on too much wine, on feeling unappreciated by an island where we had given so much. Patty was not as surprised about my behavior as I was.

The next day we returned from a dive, rinsed and hung our equipment, and gathered our personal belongings to head to lunch. "Have you seen my flip-flops?" I asked.

We all looked around. Flip-flops nowhere to be found. I began breathing hard and in anguish. First my cup and now my shoes.

I seethed all the way to lunch, and promptly fell asleep in the golf cart.

***

I felt comatose as the boat made its way out to Black Forest. The stiffness in my neck persisted. I was glad when it was time to end the dive. When I got to the surface, I struggled with the choppy water. It took only seconds to beat me up. I floated on my back, waiting for help. The stiffness in my neck persisted, leaving me abnormally fatigued.

As we motored to the last dive of the day, Mackie, our divemaster for years, looked me over. "You need a day off, my friend. No diving tomorrow. Get some rest. We're going over to English Point, and we'll keep this dive nice and easy."

An hour passed. Time to surface. The ache in my upper back became distracting. I waved my arms and hands wildly in attempts to shake off the stiffness. As I swam to the boat, the pain went lower. It felt like someone was jabbing and twisting a tire iron in my shoulder "wings." I hadn't experienced pain like that since I'd had my routine gallbladder attacks almost ten years earlier. As I reached for the line for my safety stop, I breathed harder to catch my breath. *How strange*, I thought. *I hardly exerted any effort. How can I be this tired and achy? I really need that day off."*

At lunch, my head almost fell into my plate. I needed a nap.

"Let's get you to a massage," Patty said. "Maybe that will help your stiffness."

After ninety minutes of massage, I was exhausted. Patty went out to float in the calm warm sea while I fell off for a desperately needed nap. Getting comfortable was impossible. The tire iron returned to my back. I sat up, unable to find any position that could bring even temporary comfort.

Patty returned to the room and studied my predicament. "We need to get you to the hospital."

I called my travel insurance company, the Divers Alert Network (DAN). They, too, advised me to get to the hospital.

Patty had trouble steering while holding me in the golf cart.

At the hospital, staff rushed out with a wheelchair.

The hospital was quiet. Very few patients and no one in the

emergency room but me. I found myself surrounded by nurses—one asking questions, one trying to make me comfortable, one standing waiting to help as needed, and another who ran off to find the doctor. We put them in touch with DAN, whose medical team maintained communication with the hospital staff until the doctor arrived.

They gave me morphine. The pain stopped. At last the back pain subsided. They took blood and rushed off to the lab. They gave me more morphine. Breathing once again became difficult. I struggled to sit up. "I can't breathe." I felt like I was sucking air through a straw just after finishing a race.

They placed a mask over my face for more oxygen. I gasped. Could not get enough no matter how hard I sucked. "What's wrong with me?"

"You're having a heart attack."

"You mean I'm having one right now? Or do you mean I already had one?"

"You're having one right now. You have the enzyme that confirms it."

I fell back in the bed. Breathing difficulty increased. An elephant was standing on my chest. I slipped in and out of consciousness. I was hot. I was chilled. I shivered. I sweated profusely. I kicked off the covers, then asked for them again plus more.

"Don't you die on me!" yelled Patty in my face.

I squeezed her hand and looked into her eyes. This was it. *It's out of our hands.*

Two years earlier I had sat holding my mother's hand as she took her last breaths. "Come on, Ma, get one more in there." She labored as she attempted to take one more breath. She grimaced as if in a panic or pain, and then her body relaxed.

Am I on my last ten breaths? Will I panic when the last one comes and my heart starves for oxygen and no more is on its way?

I looked at the nurses. They just stood there, witnessing a person dying. *Please, do something!*

We always think the cavalry will come to save the day, but none were coming. They say you die alone, no matter who surrounds you. Now I know what they mean. No one could help me or alter the course. I *was* on my last ten breaths. Those nurses were no longer there to keep me alive, but to ease my suffering and fear about death.

Nine breaths left.

I can't die. What a mess I'll be leaving Patty. Hold on. You can get past this.

Eight.

I'm wasting my air. I'm breathing too hard, and soon the darkness will come and I will fade away as that tear drips out of the corner of my eye.

Seven.

This all seemed to be happening so quickly. There was no time to prepare, to say goodbye, to be afraid. Maybe as I prepared my mother to die a few years before, I was preparing myself as well. I was not feeling any fear.

Six.

The choice of death was not mine. I was not part of the decision about my future anymore.

Five.

Death is an interesting phase. We fear it until we realize that struggling won't stop it, postpone it, cheat it, scare it away. Then we find peace in knowing that our struggles with health, and bill paying, and fretting over injured relationships, and people trying to cheat and steal from us will soon be over. What was so important moments ago "don't mean crap."

Four.

What mattered most was that Patty was nearby. My eyes welled up whenever I looked into hers.

Then, it seemed like the worst of my heart storm had passed. The morphine took care of the pain. My breathing returned to normal. I sat up. "Can I go home now?"

Ha! Death can be cheated after all.

They wouldn't let me go. I drifted in and out of consciousness most of the night. I had no sense of time. Air Evac was coming as soon as they could put together the medical team, get a fast plane that could fly the 1,200-mile round-trip, and clear US Homeland Security.

Patty was sent back to the room to pack up everything that could fit into a backpack or small carry-on. "What about the rest of our things?" The plane would not accommodate more than a small carry-on. Everything else would have to be handled later. She drove back in the dark along the streets gone asleep. Patty put herself in first responder mode. There was no time to be afraid, cry, or run around in circles.

At the hotel, Patty collected what was needed and left to return to the hospital. On her way out, she passed the closed-down bar where she could see Nadjet behind the barred windows counting the nightly receipts. Nadjet looked at Patty and knew instantly something was not right. She quickly drove Patty back to the hospital. "Don't worry about anything here," Nadjet said. "We'll take care of it." Soothing words Patty needed to hear. She was not alone in this mess, but she remained shackled by emotional shock.

Stateside hang-ups delayed the emergency medical machine. My body was kept calm with frequent squirts of morphine. Island visitors came—owners Jenny and Loren, dive shop owner Dale, hotel food manager Nadjet, and front-desk manager Graffy. All assured me I would be all right and told us not to worry about any of our left-behind belongings.

Five men authoritatively walked into the hospital room. They surrounded me, thumped me, listened to my heart, took my vitals, gave me more morphine, told me not to move. They lamented the delay, saying it only weakened my chance for full recovery. They strapped me on a board and slid me into the island's only ambulance. I knew where we were by each curve. I felt the hot sun and ocean breeze as they stuffed me into the small Lear jet. *Will I ever know the island sensations again?* The doctor asked me a question. I knew the answer but could not speak. He smiled, said, "Looks like the morphine's working," and gave me another shot of it. I watched the faces of the medics as they read EKGs. Thought I saw a look of concern. "How am I doing?"

"You have a long way to go to get out of the woods. You're still in great danger."

Jesus. I didn't think I was in any "great danger." This really wasn't a heart attack. A panic attack, maybe, but not a heart attack. But panic attacks don't justify sending a team of medical personnel on a private jet. The event felt the same as those gallbladder attacks that had plagued me for years, but they had passed. *Can't this heart attack just "pass"? I'm only seventy-four years old—way too young to have a debilitating illness. There's too much to see and do. This can't end. Yes, I gasped for air in the hospital, but they took care of that with medication. Whatever is wrong can be fixed, and life will go on as normal.*

We got through immigration in the States faster than I had ever known.

I found myself looking up at a team of cardiologists at a hospital in Aventura, Florida. "Looks like you've had a heart attack," one of them said. "We're going to go in and see what happened. Most likely you have a clogged artery. Luckily, it wasn't the coronary artery known as the 'widow maker'; otherwise you probably would have died under water. We'll insert a catheter and install up to three stents. If more are needed, you'll undergo bypass surgery. When you wake up, you'll know right away what we did."

I woke up what seemed like moments later. They had inserted one stent… one lousy stent. That's all it took to take care of all that trouble. They tucked me into a cardiac ICU cubbyhole and hooked tubes and wires to all parts. I was awake, but unable to move or speak.

Patty took a taxi to a hotel. She dragged our carry-on up to the room where the only welcome was darkness and the low din of the air conditioner. She sat on the bed, exhausted and spent. For her, the great life-changing emotional ordeal was over for the day. She no longer needed to be in first responder mode. She fell back onto the bed and began sobbing. She sobbed and sobbed and sobbed until she fell asleep.

I spent days in the ICU and had only one midnight emotional meltdown as my nurse sat holding my hand and brought ice cream, the miracle food for such occasions. She encouraged me to talk. "I do not fear death," I said. "I fear running out of life before I die, and I fear this heart attack will do that to me. Just yesterday, it seems, I was immortal. When did it change? How did it happen so fast? How did it come to this?"

She remained sitting close to my bed and holding my hand, patting me when it sounded like I was about to go into another emotional tailspin. She said nothing during a time when holding someone's hand and saying nothing is the best thing to do.

I spent a few weeks in Aventura waiting for clearance to travel. Patty found a nearby mall and used it for an escape. She walked, she shopped, she took me for short walks, she kept my family informed, and she kept everyone calm.

The resort owner, Jenny, and dive shop owner, Dale, packed our equipment. Three weeks later all of it arrived unharmed.

My heart attack was considered mild as these events go. It took months to recover enough to make it through a day without sleeping through most of it. It took a year for me to regain my confidence in that all-important piece of machinery called a heart. How come we have two of everything else?

Three months after the heart event, my cardiologist—also a scuba diver—cleared me for diving. He told me I could resume diving—nothing stressful and nothing deep. Two weeks later we headed to Grand Turk. It was good to be back home.

The entire ordeal cost almost $200,000 in medical expenses, including that $22,000 airplane ride where they would not allow me to sit up and see the marble-blue swirling sand in the Bahama Banks below. Excluding the cost of travel insurance, my out-of-pocket expense was less than $50. Is this not the best business case for not leaving home without insurance?

We nervously chuckle about death and say, "When it's your time, it's your time." We think about dying more than *where* we die. Some people shuddered when they heard my heart attack occurred at fifty feet. What does it matter? When it's your time, it's your time. Death itself matters more than *where* it comes.

Medical events change people. I'm no exception. I don't get upset like before. Is the cost of being angry really worth it in the end?

When you lose your balance and begin to fall, the first thing you do is drop whatever you're holding. When I got close to death, I dropped everything and reached for what was most important to me—Patty's hand. Nothing matters except the health of the relationships we have with loved ones. And the rest of the world? Nothing.

DOLPHINS ON MY BUCKET LIST

DIVE LOG

Date: August 2021
Location: Amphitheatre—Grand Turk, Turks and Caicos

Swimming with dolphins has never been on my bucket list. Why jump in if all I would see are fins swimming away?

Thanks to diving with a professional photographer thirty-five years ago, I learned how to get up close and personal with most creatures in Planet Ocean. By approaching fish from below, allowing them to get used to me, and breathing slowly, I could be among them. I didn't need this technique with encounters with dolphins, sea lions, or other ocean-dwelling mammals. Don't bother with slow breathing and slow moving... If they are curious, they don't hesitate to come close. If you get a chance to touch them, it's only on their terms.

At Grand Turk, we have seen small pods of dolphins swimming in the shallows and have attempted to position the boat in their path, hoping to be in the water when they pass. I have had my share of dolphin encounters. I have enjoyed the privilege of being with them but have never been with anyone who can compete with the excitement Patty exhibits when there is a possibility of an encounter.

I discovered the power of GoPro video. Through their software, I discovered I could watch video pictures and produce the perfect accidental head-on still shot. During each dive trip, I took dozens of hours of video and realized I was repeatedly taking pictures of the same creatures. How many photos of French grunts does one need? Although it was fun, it took thrice the hours to sift through them as it had to take them. I found something more interesting in the water and turned my video attention to Patty, who was perhaps the most graceful diver I have ever seen.

When water temperatures approached 84–85 degrees, we dove without wet suits. Patty and I decided we should make photo journals that only we would view when our diving days were over and all we had were memories of "back in the day." When sharing the boat with strangers, getting a topless mermaid Patty in and out of the water presented logistical challenges. We discovered a good compromise with a sheer dive shirt. As divers prepared for the dive, Patty turned her back to the group and swapped her swim top for the dive shirt.

After returning from a dive, Patty was standing at the stern of the boat to change when the divemaster yelled, "Dolphins! Right under the boat. Quick! Grab your mask and get in or you'll miss them."

Instantly the boat emptied except for the divemaster. The other swimmers chased the dolphin's tails while Patty swam furiously to where she anticipated they would go. I couldn't keep up with her. When the dolphins were gone, only Patty could say she had had an encounter.

The divemaster picked up the group and then motored toward us. Everyone on the boat talked at once about what they had almost seen. The boat pulled up to us and Patty climbed the ladder. She stood waving her arms and "yahooing" about swimming with dolphins. Her enthusiasm distracted the others, who stopped talking, turned to the zesty diver, and stood gaping at a very excited Patty. We never learned if their dinner talks that night were about "almost seen" dolphins or mermaids.

We resumed our photo sessions and collected enough material over the years to create a Shutterfly book of fish and mermaids. We lamented that we had no photos of Patty swimming with dolphins—with or without a top.

The summer of 2021 arrived, and the island remained almost devoid of diving tourists because of COVID-19 pandemic restrictions. We had the boat to ourselves for most of our monthlong holiday—perfect for unbridled photo opportunities.

The dive site, Amphitheatre, was about midway between both ends of the island and had predictably good visibility. It had an interesting wall and plenty of coral heads to explore in the sand shallows during the last half of the dive.

We surfaced and boarded the boat, talking about the great dive. The divemaster pulled up the anchor and began a short ride to another dive site. He pointed to the south and calmly said, "Dolphins."

Patty jumped with enthusiasm. "Which way are they headed?"

"They're coming our way," said the divemaster as he calculated where to intercept them. "Get your snorkels and fins on and prepare for a backward roll over the side when I tell you. They're close to the boat! Get in now!"

We rolled over the side just as three dolphins swam directly below us. Patty and I were separated by about fifty feet, and I could hear her cheering through her snorkel. No sooner were we in the water than the dolphin encounter ended. We were lucky to see what we did, even though all I saw were dolphin fins swimming away. Can that even count as a dolphin encounter?

A hundred or so feet away was our boat. The divemaster was leaning over the boat, petting one of the dolphins whose head was out of the water. It sank and swam toward Patty, who stroked it as it slowly swam past her. I turned on the video to capture what I could. The animal turned its attention and swam slowly on the surface toward me.

My first reaction was to get out of its way, but what good would that do if Mr. Dolphin was on a ramming mission? Its slow approach told me I was in no danger but had to remain cautious—I was being approached by a large and powerful "wild" animal with "unpredictable behavior." It slowed more as it came within a few feet. Was that a smile on its face? How can an approaching dolphin with a face like that be "wild" and "unpredictable"?

Do not touch a dolphin unless it initiates contact, were the words I recalled from articles. I kept my hands to myself although all I wanted to do was take the opportunity to touch it.

It swam closer and more slowly. It buried its nose in my chest and gently nudged. There was no misreading its moves… I was being invited to touch. I stroked the top of its head, its back, and its fins. It was smooth, unlike the sandpaper skin of sharks. It changed positions and put its head out of the water and looked at me. I wrapped my arm around it as it slowly began to swim away. My video was rolling, and I quickly lengthened the selfie stick and got a video of the dolphin, this wild and unpredictable beast, with me at its side.

Moments later the dolphin was gone.

Back on the boat, Patty stood waving her arms, smiling broadly, excited over swimming with dolphins. I had captured the event of a genuine dolphin encounter, but it was without the requisite mermaid needed for the photo album.

"This is not what dolphins typically do," I said to the divemaster. "What do you make of it?"

"We've had these encounters with this dolphin before. We think it's the offspring of one that was in captivity, maybe from Nassau. One time another divemaster said he saw the dolphin slapping its tail three times before swimming away."

When the divemaster had positioned the boat in front of the animals, I had not planned to jump in. I knew all I would see, if anything, would be fins and tails of passing dolphins. What drove me to roll in I don't know, but had I remained on the boat, I would have missed the most dramatic encounter with these creatures of the sea in forty years of diving.

I was always one to grab the moment when the opportunity presented itself. Many people have told me I move too fast, that the moment I seize may be more harmful than what I imagined. Sometimes my aging body tells me to watch and the kid inside says to "go for it. My encounter with the dolphin drove home the point that a person can sit in the bleachers and watch the game or jump in and become a part of it. I believe that's when the extraordinary memories are made.

I'LL BE RIGHT BACK

Chris McLaughlin stood next to me on the boat platform as I readied myself for dive number 700. He prepared two signs—one for me with "700" printed on it, and one for him, dive 7,000. He shook my hand, took a celebratory picture, made a big deal of my accomplishment, and taught me how important it is to be mindful when standing next to someone jumping around with excitement as they celebrate dive 70.

* * *

Two octopuses hid from this intruder until they thought it safe to extend their tentacles in their search for each other. When their pencil-thin tentacles touched, they intertwined and caressed each other with the gentleness of a pussy-willow bud. If there was ever a time when I felt like a trespasser in the world below, that was it.

I rescued a small crab from a footprint-sized tide pool. It gave its best fight, but in my persistence I saved it from the water that was quickly warming under the hot sun. I carefully set it free in the cooling waters of a larger pool. I watched it drift down, down, down into the hungry mouth of a sea anemone that quickly engulfed it. The little crab was never seen by human eyes again. I thought I was acting to rescue the critter, but in retrospect it appeared to be for the satisfaction of being the rescuer. Some lessons are easy but come at the terrible expense of others.

* * *

The journey is one of discovery. We see what we want. We see beauty or ugliness, joy or sadness, love or hate, anger or peace. Although experiences are pleasant or harsh, lessons are always sent for those who are willing to learn. They never fail to strengthen human character.

* * *

I have shared my lessons through these stories, and there are many others from untold anecdotes. Through my journeys, some lessons were bricks on my head. Others were less obvious, such as these takeaways:

- *Blame never improves the results*—I found myself on the north coast of Oahu, Hawaii, in bad water fighting a losing battle. Soon I would drown. My spouse was thousands of miles away, unaware how close she was to becoming a widow. The divemaster said I had enough experience to be there. He was wrong, but it was me who was drowning.

- *The quest for human power ends at sea level*—The laws of nature are quite simple. They are without discussion, legal debate, or interpretation. In Planet Ocean, it is not about power, glory, who owns or rules what, who is more superior, or who has more trophies. Political games do not exist. No creature will honor your visit. No one tries to outdo the other. There are no bullies. There is no "getting even." There are no rules about dominion. Instead, they are simple. It's all about food. Bigger creatures eat smaller ones. Down in the deep I am safe, spared from the danger that waits when it is time to surface.

- *Economics doesn't make the better culture*—Although our technologies may be superior, we seem to have become so caught up in them that we begin to believe that we have it all over the deprived or less fortunate. My attraction to developing countries lies in being connected to a common sense of community and family values that protected me as a child. So what became of them, those old values? I believe they were forsaken for financial security and career position. Nothing wrong with that except some of us got a little greedy. There's hope when we immerse ourselves in a culture of warmth, honesty, and selflessness—such as what I found in developing countries.

- *If we are entitled to anything, it's gotta be emotional freedom—*Sarah cowered in tears on French Beach. She washed out of the program. Was told by her husband to come home scuba certified or not at all. With luck, she found the door locked when she got back that Sunday night. I find too many people living a stifled existence under the heel of spineless bullies. When I felt the taste of fresh air that comes with freedom, it became my mission to encourage others to discover its flavor for themselves. Be wary of bullies. Although most of them run when punched back, some hang tough to finish you off.

- *The demons that visit us never come uninvited—*Not all our choices are good ones. Some are downright irrational. Remembering our poor choices helps us better understand our children. And ourselves. I gazed into the mirror. I saw myself—the good, the bad, and the ugly. It can be very painful. I convinced myself I deserved nothing good, and when a good companion appeared in my window, she became my most regrettable lost love. Bad choices beget bad choices, and when I was facedown on the sidewalk, a gentle voice in my angry head told me it was time to get up and come home. I packed my things and sent the demons into the deep, but not without a ceremony that nearly took me into the abyss with them. It was a defining moment. How easy it was to send them away, and how clever and deceptive they were in convincing me they should stay.

- *Dominion is a responsibility, not an entitlement—*Man's sense of dominion over the world is a show of arrogance. If you cringe over discussions about spirituality, skip this section. Justification for human primacy over animals came from religions that said humans are superior to animals because they have an immortal soul, and that God commanded humans to rule over animals. I grew up under the notion that people were smart and the animal kingdom was not. A large pod of dolphins, about a thousand in number, turned in unison and headed in our direction. How did they communicate and choreograph their moves? Why did the dolphin turn away from his pod and initiate a connection with me? God gave man an intellect, which can be more of a liability than an asset, especially when impaired by dormancy, hatred, or blinding ambition. Mother Nature gave wildlife survival techniques at birth, and somehow they live in harmony and balance. Don't you wish we could? I believe we can if we choose to observe with an open mind. This lesson was among the pile of bricks on my head. When I turned to the "dominated" world for a new perspective, I began respecting its delicate nature and accepted my responsibility to protect it and, most importantly, view all things as mentors.

- *We don't own the world*—It ain't ours. It has been entrusted to us. We must be caretakers, not takers. We must leave our mark through contribution, not depletion. What we do today we owe to the past and the future. This was a harsh lesson for me to learn because what I criticize here I most likely did in an earlier life.

- *When it is time to get off the stage, we have to either get off or get shoved off*—Sometimes we stay in our light too long because of pride, and that could hurt others. I was a hotshot scuba instructor. My profession took me away from it, and I got soft and rusty. I retained my certification so I could teach my granddaughter to dive. Did I want her to experience Planet Ocean like I had or did I want my name on her certification card? Pride. It is best to get off the stage gracefully and become a mentor.

- *Purposelessness is curable*—I was there in 1988 when we christened a new dive site. By 2003 it had been renamed, and the history of my past had been erased. How embittering and emotionally disemboweling. There will always be a younger generation inheriting or taking over the world. They fearlessly and recklessly change the landscape and rewrite history. They cast aside those who carved the path on which they stand. They know me not for who I am or what I was. Now I am too old and slow to participate in the race and have been discarded because of a lack of perceived value. Welcome to the club. The longer I wallow in self-pity for having a crushed legacy, the faster I will succumb to the most debilitating disease plaguing mankind—a sense of purposelessness. In the end, no one cares what I did or what I had, but ideally they do care about who I am. Long ago I listened to a sermon about miracles, that they continue to happen all the time and we can get in on the process by being someone's angel. A kind word can breathe new life into a despondent person. A word of encouragement can change the course of a person's life. Giving someone something to believe in can light them on fire with inspiration. A little empathy is the best connection to others. So when I'm old and no one remembers me for what I used to do, I think I'll just shuffle over to someone and be an angel with a kind word. This is the best antidote for purposelessness.

- *We all come from the same cloth*—I saved this one for the end. To me, it is the magic and miracle of connection. There is a common denominator among all beings—we seek to be worthwhile, valued, and important. We want to matter and feel purposeful. If we don't, we tend to misbehave. Understanding this is the greatest lesson in finding a path to interpersonal relationships. Understand this and you're "home free."

This is what I wrote in the first edition:

> *I'm off to collect more stories about good people, great cultures, sea creatures, fair maidens, mermaids, and other sea beasts. My biological grandfather was Bermuda born. I heard he was a sea captain of tall ships and had a wanderlust that took him away before he had a chance to introduce himself to my mother. I am off to join a ship as crew to sail there from the Virgin Islands. His stuff is in my blood. I want to find him. I'll be right back.*

In 2010 I joined as crew to sail from the British Virgin Islands to Chesapeake Bay. Wave after wave of low-pressure weather fronts extended our eight-day trip to a grueling and dangerous fifteen-day ordeal. When a few fifteen-foot waves broke over our stern, the captain looked to the northeast and yelled, "You up to holing up in Bermuda?"

"I heard my biological grandfather lived there. It could be a family reunion. Let's go."

We never made Bermuda. Instead, we remained hove-to in our sailboat for two days and got pushed a hundred miles off course. Bermuda in search of unknown relatives is now out of the question—I have had too many birthdays to pilot a ship. Be that as it may, this great journey of mine is not over. Not until my last breath.

NOTHING IS FOREVER

I'm no fool.
Nothing is forever.
Not here anyway.
Eventually all trails lead back to dust
When Mother Earth takes back what's hers.
It is the way of it.

A person's worth is not measured by the cover,
But in the quality of the stuff in between.
Good stories are authored in the will.
In the will of one with good spirit.

Love stories come where exists a dream.
A romantic one is best.
Ah, the dream…
It shines strong.
Even when there's only a flicker.
I know
It does for me.
It always did.
Goodbye.

www.ingramcontent.com/pod-product-compliance
Lightning Source LLC
Chambersburg PA
CBHW031244290426
44109CB00012B/428